"As I read *With Fresh Eyes*, I felt like I was the one seeing for the first time. Karen Wingate's vivid descriptions, poignant insights, and overwhelming awe of God's goodness opened my eyes to the evidence of God's presence all around me. She dusts the world for God's fingerprints and finds them everywhere. Then she invites us to marvel with her as we see our world anew."

LORI HATCHER, author of *Refresh Your Faith*

"*With Fresh Eyes* is a true spiritual treasure. Writing with a deep faith and a transparency forged in the fire of trials, Karen Wingate opens our eyes to the many wonders of the life of faith: patience, hope, trust, contentment, and gratitude, to name a few. Her personal stories and practical application will challenge you to see God and his work from a new perspective."

SHAWN McMULLEN, vice president of partner relations for the Christian Church Leadership Foundation, and author of *Coming Home to Holiness*

"In this thoughtful and beautifully written book, Karen Wingate provides a refreshing perspective on life's challenges, renewed vision, and God's faithfulness."

CANDY ARRINGTON, author of *Life on Pause*

"Rather than focusing on her miraculous recovery of sight, Wingate invites her readers to see God's miracles all around them. It is, indeed, an eye-opening book!"

JAMES N. WATKINS, award-winning author, speaker, and editor of *Intimacy with Christ*

"Karen Wingate's warm, personal messages are deeply relatable yet challenged me to look at things in a different way. I'm grateful for that. Gazing at life through fresh eyes, I was amazed at her perspective and revelations."

CECIL MURPHEY, author or coauthor of 140 books, including *Gifted Hands: The Ben Carson Story*

WITH
FRESH
EYES

WITH FRESH EYES

60 Insights *into the Miraculously Ordinary*
from a Woman Born Blind

Karen Wingate

KREGEL
PUBLICATIONS

Cataloging-in-Publication Data is available from the Library of Congress.

ISBN 978-0-8254-4681-8, print
ISBN 978-0-8254-7728-7, epub

Printed in the United States of America
21 22 23 24 25 26 27 28 29 30 / 5 4 3 2 1

To Karen (Fergy) Ferguson,
who dared to believe in
Better Than Ever

Contents

Part 3: Seeing What God Wants Me to See

Part 4: Seeing Who God Wants Me to See

Part 5: The Good, the Ugly, and the Ordinary

Part 6: Seeing Beyond the Seen

Introduction

*I remain confident of this: I will see the goodness of
the Lord in the land of the living. Wait for the Lord;
be strong and take heart and wait for the Lord.*
—PSALM 27:13–14

Labeled as legally blind since infancy, I wished I could see as others saw, but I never allowed myself to think it possible. At birth, my eyes opened to a veil as thick as an industrial-strength shower curtain liner. Eight childhood surgeries cleared my vision enough to read textbooks three inches from my heavy bifocals and chalkboards from the front row.

That was out of my good left eye. The only thing my severely crossed right eye could see was a fuzzy image of the bridge of my nose. Ninety percent of the time, I looked at life through my dominant left eye. Those surgeries gave me some functional vision but caused damage in other ways that compromised the overall health of my eyes.

With a growing catalog of problems and risks, I knew deep within that the day might come when my sight would further diminish. Early on, I determined to make the most of what vision I had until God and aging chose otherwise. Yet, like accepting any aging process or terminal illness, we're never quite ready to hear that things are getting worse faster than we thought.

Then the unimaginable happened. In my midfifties, a random surgery to fix one of my latest issues gave me brand-new eyesight.

Today, I see a world I have never seen before. Birds, clouds, flowers, and numbers on the bathroom scale tattle on what I've missed. I see the smiles of loved ones, recognize friends halfway across a room, and take Communion without someone handing me the emblems. My visual discoveries opened the eyes of my soul and convinced me beyond a doubt of the existence of a God who has the power and creativity to make an intricate and complex world. A God who possesses such lavish, personal love that he would bestow the gift of sight on one middle-aged woman and teach her to see his beloved children as he sees them. A God who promises to stay with us through the unlit moments of earthly life and lead us to the land where there is no shadow of darkness. A God who has made it simple (but not always easy) for us to see him.

I invite you to watch with me and see how God can walk this journey with you too. See how he can be more amazing than we ever dared to hope. Whisper to him, *Give me a fresh look at life, Lord.* And then come see a world God created for no other reason than that he wanted to do it for you. Rediscover the blessing of seeing the good, bad, and what we call the ugly or ordinary. Recapture the longing to see Jesus in all his goodness, love, and power. Allow him to remove the veil over your heart so you can see him as he truly is.

Are you ready? Like the Old Testament prophet Moses, do you want to see more than a glimmer of his glory (Exod. 33:18)? Or like the psalmist's penned heart cry, do you long for a dew-kissed drop of his intimacy (Ps. 42:1)? Are you ready to hold God's hand and let him guide you on an incredible journey toward the discovery of who he is? He will not disappoint you. In fact, you may be overwhelmed with the enormity of his creativity, orderliness, and sheer goodness.

I know I was.

So, come join me. Together, let's watch God do the impossible and worship in wonder at how he can make us strong while we wait for his perfect timing. I've got front-row seats reserved for both of us.

No, not the front row. For you see, I don't need to sit in the front row anymore. Let's go find seats in the middle.

Let's go look for God together.

PART 1

THOSE WALKING IN DARKNESS . . .

Bed Covers

"What do you want me to do for you?"
"Lord, I want to see," he replied.
—LUKE 18:41

"Watch carefully. This is a day you will always remember."

My grandfather's voice spoke behind me as I sat crossed-legged three feet from our thirteen-inch black-and-white television. It was July 20, 1969, the day Neil Armstrong stepped onto the moon's surface. We watched and heard him utter, "That's one small step for man, one giant leap for mankind."

It's a pivotal day seared into my memory. Mankind may have leaped forward, but I was stuck. At nine years of age, I was old enough to realize my limited vision made me different from other children and that the final eye surgery of my childhood, done three days before Armstrong's step on the moon's surface, had not improved my sight enough to make a noticeable difference.

Still despondent two mornings later, I vented my frustration to my mother. She turned her back on me, faced a sink full of dishes, and murmured words I strained to hear. "God can do miracles, Karen."

Miracles happen only in the Bible, I wanted to sneer. That's what our conservative church taught despite long prayer lists intoned by the minister each Sunday. Yet, if my mother said miracles were possible and Preacher Carl prayed for the healing of the sick, why not? Surgery hadn't cured my eyes; perhaps God could.

With the innocence of a nine-year-old who didn't know how these things work, and without consulting anyone on how it should be done, I started the next day with a prayer. As my sleepy brain dragged itself into consciousness, I pulled the covers tightly over my head and squeezed my eyes shut against the glare of the morning sun. "Please, God. I want to see. Let this be the day I see better." I relinquished the covers and opened my eyes.

No change.

I wasn't giving up.

I prayed the next morning. And the next. For almost two weeks, I repeated the ritual, my enthusiasm waning each time. Soon I skipped a day, then another, and then several days in a row. God wasn't answering. Or so I thought.

Why didn't he?

I've pondered those summer weeks many times. What if God had granted me 20/20 vision that first Monday morning when the world was enamored with three astronauts? A nine-year-old child with genetically malfunctioning eyes healed instantly. Who would have learned of the miracle? Who would have believed it? It might have caused a stir within our church, among our neighborhood friends, and in my school, but the memory of the miracle would have faded and everyone would have gone on with their lives. In my youthful eagerness, I too would have forgotten that once upon a time, I could not see.

I gave up praying for healing, but I didn't give up on God. Was it the Holy Spirit who amended my prayer? "Lord, help me get through life with poor eyesight." That prayer God honored in ways a watching community could hardly fathom. One social worker described me as having more "functional vision than any of our other visually impaired clients." In the ensuing decades, God proved trustworthy in his ability to safely lead me along paths I could not see. And during those years, he must have smiled behind his divine hand, knowing that forty-six years later, he would have ready an answer to my prayer that would surprise and delight me and everyone around me.

God never promised to answer your prayers the moment you ask, he promised he would answer.

God never promised to answer your prayers the moment you ask; he promised he would answer. Sometimes he will grant your request immediately; other times he responds, not according to your limited understanding of your needs but in his way with his wisdom. God gives, not necessarily what you think you want, but the deepest longings of your heart, the longings he created you to have. You'll look back at that moment and say, "Oh yes, that really was what I wanted most."

In the interim, he'll give you the chance to become your best, sculpting your heart's desire to be in tandem with his best for you. And unseen by you and me, he's gathering our audience, so when the time comes, a watching world will see our story and give glory to the Giver.

Sadly, impatient to receive the end at the beginning, we often chafe at God's seemingly slow pace or at what we perceive as his misunderstanding of what we want. It's easy to feel like the psalmist David: "How long, LORD? Will you forget me forever? How long will you hide your face from me?" (Ps. 13:1). The revealing of God's plans and promises is a process. God waits and works with us, equipping us to use the gift he is preparing for us and teaching us contentment with the presence of the Giver more than the pleasure of the gift.

What do you want? Go deeper. What do you really want? How badly do you want it? Enough to allow the Lord to choose how and when you receive the gift? Until God chooses to give you what you want most, let the Lord know you are willing to be content with what he has given you for this moment.

The psalmist gives the answer to this season of waiting: "But I trust in your unfailing love; my heart rejoices in your salvation. I will sing the LORD's praise, for he has been good to me" (Ps. 13:5–6).

Do you find it hard to wait? Tell God you are willing to trust that he knows the best timing, that he's walking with you in the meantime, and that, to this point, he has been so very good to you.

Lord, help me work with you in the wait so I will be at my best when your answer comes. Prepare me so I can be ready to acknowledge you as the Giver of the gift.

SEEING WITH FRESH EYES

Name what you would like most to see happen in your life. Ask God for it, telling him you are willing to wait and receive his gift in the way and time he sees fit.

2

Brown Curtain

*My hand will sustain him; surely my arm will
strengthen him.*
—PSALM 89:21

*D*espite my childhood prayer for healing, I spent my life labeled as legally blind. Mercifully, my vision remained stable and God empowered me to adapt to normal life with low vision. Was it easy? I won't hedge. No, it wasn't. But I determined to make the most of every day and the best of what I had. I threw myself into marriage, motherhood, and ministry, attempting things that probably left bystanders holding their breath or muttering, "Can she really do that?"

The day came when my adaptations weren't enough.

I stepped up to the podium one Sunday morning, ready to lead music for our small congregation, and looked down at my large-print lyrics cheat sheet. The words were nothing more than jumbled black lines. I looked out over the waiting congregation. Instead of the blurry faces I normally saw, I could only detect vague movements behind a brown curtain.

It was then that I knew. I was losing what precious little eyesight I had. Quickly. It was bad timing. Bad, bad. In front of a public audience, no less.

I admit, I have a stubborn streak. I wasn't about to tell the crowd, "I'm losing my vision. Can someone else lead songs?" Instead, I quipped, "Some days I see better than others, and today is not one of those days. You'll all have to sing louder so I can hear the words." *Oh, Lord Jesus, help me through the next fifteen minutes.*

For six months, I'd had a premonition that something was off. Images would look jagged, then revert to normal blurriness. I didn't tell anyone because I didn't want to appear obsessed about something that was nothing. Can you relate? I waited till my next visit with my ophthalmologist and casually mentioned the oddity. She arranged for me to see a retina specialist, "just to be on the safe side." The specialist found a retinal tear that looked months old and probably beyond surgical repair.

"Let's check again in three months," he said.

Fine by me. With a catalog of eye issues and risk factors, and the aging process, I had lived with the knowledge that the day would come when I could lose more eyesight. If jagged waves were the extent of the visual change, I could live with that.

But as my next checkup neared, my vision didn't look normal. Every life activity took more effort, and I found myself increasingly frustrated with how I was seeing my world. The Sunday of the brown-curtain eyesight was four days before my next appointment.

The retina specialist confirmed my suspicions. The tear had grown. It was time for surgery.

"I can't promise anything," he said. "Your vision might be better than it is now or it might not change at all. It could be worse. But I'll do the best I can."

I knew my medical history well enough to understand the possibilities. My eyeball structure was so fragile, any invasive measures were a risk.

The prospect of vision loss is scary. In talking with people, I've noticed that vision loss ranks near the top of what people fear most. And we're never ready for a crisis when it actually happens, whether it's losing our vision, watching our bank account hit zero, or sitting at the bedside of a loved one who's losing their battle to a terminal illness. The moment it happens is never a good moment.

How do you face unavoidable crisis?

Jesus came to this earth to die a sinner's death. He knew his mission. He knew a horrifying death waited. Yet, on the night before his death, he knelt alone in a garden called Gethsemane, his three closest friends asleep, clueless about what the next day held. Jesus stared that moment in the face. It's happening. Now. The tread of soldiers' feet, those who would arrest him, sounded on the cobblestone streets, closer, closer.

"Father, if you are willing, take this cup from me," he cried (Luke 22:42).

None of us want to walk through the hard moments, even Jesus. Yet Jesus shows us how to cope. While honest about his preferences, he also articulated his willingness to do things God's way: "Not my will, but yours be done" (v. 42).

I don't like losing my vision; you don't like the hard moment you face. God never expects us to suck it up and suffer silently when we encounter those agonizing seasons of life. But as Jesus affirmed in the garden, our commitment to do things God's way, even when it's not our preference, shouts our belief in two central truths.

First, he is God and we are not. He knows what he is doing even if we don't see it. He sees the big picture and we cannot.

God hears your Gethsemane cry.

Second, God hears your Gethsemane cry. The next verse in Jesus's story tells how an angel appeared and strengthened him (Luke 22:43). God will show the same care for you. He will strengthen you so you can make it to the other side of the crisis.

What gave me the inner strength to move forward in that instant on the church podium? God had sustained me so many times over the decades of my life. If he had done it before, he could do it again. So as the music began, I prayed furiously for God's grace to get me through. The congregation sang loud enough for my mind to fill in the words I could not see, and the brown curtain lifted enough for me to find my seat afterward.

God had strengthened and sustained, just as he said he would.

Lord, I thank you for the ways you have cared for
me, and I trust that as you have done in the past,
so you will continue to do.

SEEING WITH FRESH EYES

Make a list of three times God has sustained you in the past. Name a looming crisis you fear will happen. Tell God, "Not my will, but yours be done. I want what you want."

3

Mammogram

Let us hold unswervingly to the hope we profess,
for he who promised is faithful.
—HEBREWS 10:23

*O*beying the orders of the surgeon's assistant to clear my calendar of everything for at least two weeks, I went into overdrive, including the scheduling of an overdue mammogram. As my husband, Jack, and I left the house for a full day of errands, I checked the mail. The hospital wanted a retake on my mammogram. We paused to make a few phone calls. Details fell into place faster than I could breathe, and the next day found me sitting in a dressing cubicle after the test, waiting for the report from the radiologist, who "just happened" to be in the building that morning and could read the films right away.

Then it hit me. Less than a month before, a friend fifteen years younger than I had sat in this room and heard the news that she had aggressive breast cancer. What if the results were positive? This on top of a risky eye surgery. Worst-case scenario. Blindness and breast cancer.

I heard an echo of the enemy's sneer in the account of Job. *Sure. Karen half expects vision loss. She thinks her lifelong coping skills will carry her through. But give her cancer, make her helpless, and she'll despair.*

She'll doubt the love of her heavenly Father. She'll think she's unable to serve her God any longer.

It's a knee-jerk reaction to ask, *Why are you allowing this, God?* But I quickly realized that's the wrong question. At stake was my response to unwanted life circumstances. If I suffered both blindness and cancer, would I keep believing in a loving, reliable God? Would I stay faithful?

I have found that before God ushers us into the impossible, he brings us to an intersection, a crucible of faith, asking these key questions: *If the worst happened, would you still trust me? Would you still represent me as a good God? Would you still choose to make right choices based on your belief in my Word?*

Would you?

In the Bible, three Jewish men, friends of the prophet Daniel, faced that choice. A foreign king set up a monstrosity of an idol and commanded everyone to bow down and worship it. Would these three friends obey their earthly king or stay faithful to God's commands and risk certain death? That day, in the quiet of a dressing room, clutching the ridiculous hospital gown around my possibly blemished chest, the words of those committed men of God burned bright, as if from my own furnace of doom. "But if not, let it be known to you, O king, that we do not serve your gods, nor will we worship the gold image which you have set up" (Dan. 3:18 NKJV).

The detour of the moment does not determine our ultimate destination.

But if not. That was the answer. Circumstances would not dictate my trust in God. I would follow him no matter where life took me, for the detour of the moment does not determine our ultimate destination.

A knock sounded on the door of the dressing room. The radiologist had examined the X-ray films; all was clear. A week later, that random eye surgery brought results none of us anticipated. I'm grateful I didn't have to face more vision loss or breast cancer.

I'm also thankful for that defining moment when God questioned the caliber of my faith, for I am stronger with the memory that I was willing to say yes. My deliberations during those five minutes in the dressing room persuaded me that God would have provided and given me just as great a story to tell about his love and glory if I had lost rather than gained.

You and I have limits to what we can handle. We're human, fallible, and vulnerable. But God has no restrictions. The question to ask ourselves is not how much can we handle, but how much can he handle? The answer is, all of it and more besides.

Do you fear that life might give you a one-two punch? Do you question why God allows you to face your current struggles? Or deep down, do you wonder if you are strong enough to cope, fearful you might let down the Lord you love by your knee-buckling faithlessness?

God can deal with anything you face: catastrophe on top of crisis, illness and infidelity, heartache and hardship. Trust is following Jesus and refusing to cave to your own solutions even in the "but if not" circumstances. It's a kind of stubborn faith that sees the looming storm and whispers, *I will follow you, Lord, no matter what.* It's affirming that God has the power to rescue and to sustain. It's telling God before and during the crisis that even though the fires of hell reach angry fingers toward you, you will not let go of your belief in a good, good God. You will grip tight to a God who can and will bring you through the worst life has to throw at you.

This day, choose to trust God in your worst-case moment. Let him be in charge of the details of how and when he will provide. He invites you to relinquish your desire to be part of the planning process so he can give you the best outcome. Until then, he has equal power to sustain you and keep you steady through the worst of any situation.

Lord God, you are infinitely stronger than I am.
Help me trust, follow, honor, and serve you, no
matter what.

SEEING WITH FRESH EYES

Write the words "But if not" on a small piece of paper. Tuck it inside your Bible as a reminder to hold on to your faith in God no matter what happens to you.

4

Prayer Circle

Jesus looked at them and said, "With man this is impossible, but not with God; all things are possible with God."
—MARK 10:27

$\mathcal{W}$hile I waited in the dressing cubicle for the radiologist's read on my mammogram, a notification sounded on my phone. Bev had posted an announcement on our ladies' Bible study Facebook page about a prayer circle for me the night before my surgery.

When is it appropriate to arrive for a prayer meeting in your honor?

I walked through the doorway of the church five minutes before the start time, already humbled that my Bible study ladies wanted to do this for me. I wasn't prepared for the scene before me. Every seat was taken, and women were dragging more chairs into the small sitting area. A total of twenty women, some not even part of the Bible study group, gathered that night to pray for me.

The wonder kept growing. I knew these ladies personally. Every week, we gathered and shared our hearts with each other, praying through the specific moments, heartaches, and joys of our lives. I knew which women I could count on to talk and which ones I knew better than to ask to read Scripture or pray aloud. Yet that evening, every single woman prayed out loud for me. Humbled and grateful don't begin to describe my feelings. If the unity and single-hearted purpose of that prayer circle was all the good that came from my surgery, I was ecstatic.

It takes so little to please me.

One prayer put a damper on that special evening. My close friend Karen, whom we called Fergy to avoid confusion over our names, prayed that God would give me better sight than I'd ever had before. I sucked in my breath, hiding my silent laughter. I felt like Sarah in the Bible when God told her husband, Abraham, that she would bear a son in her old age (Gen. 18:11–13). Didn't Fergy know about the genetic defect, the eight childhood surgeries, and the long list of risk factors? After what my retina specialist told me, God would get the glory if my vision did nothing more than return to status quo. I wouldn't ask for more.

Looking back, I'm a bit embarrassed. Wasn't I the one who so often said God could do anything? By refusing to ask God for above and beyond what I could imagine, I was deciding for him what he could do and what he was willing to do. That should be his choice, not mine.

Yes, God reserves the right to determine what is best for us, to exchange our request for what is in our best interest. His purpose in answering our prayers is not merely to make our lives more comfortable and convenient but to show us and those watching us that he alone is God.

So when we pray for the impossible, our request tells God that we believe he is capable of doing above and beyond our human ability, that he alone is God, and that he can do this big thing. Our prayer comes with a caveat, though: "I know you can do this God, but it's okay if you choose another path. Whatever happens, I want you to get the credit for this one."

But isn't asking for the impossible kind of putting God to the test? I still thought as Fergy prayed. Asking God for Better Than Ever vision seemed like it was demanding too much of a benevolent God who had already richly blessed my life. I wasn't going to test God like that.

My reaction sounded like a Bible character named King Ahaz.

The Bible tells how the prophet Isaiah challenged the king one day: "Ask the LORD your God for a sign, whether in the deepest depths or in the highest heights" (Isa. 7:11).

Deepest depths or highest heights? Are you serious, Isaiah?

King Ahaz turned down the offer. "I will not ask," he said. "I will not put the LORD to the test" (v. 12).

I've heard it said different ways. Haven't you?

I don't want to bother God.

I should focus on my blessings instead of asking God for more.

Others have more important needs than I do.

Really?

God wants to bless his children with good gifts, but we can be so stubbornly self-sufficient. He wants to show us and those around us the awesome impossible he can do.

Isaiah upped the ante. You want something impossible, Ahaz? Try a virgin birth (Isa. 7:14). A woman bearing a child who will bring God to, with, and within his people. How much more impossible can you get than that?

Why not ask big and bold? You never know what God might have waiting for you.

Why not ask big and bold? You never know what God might have waiting for you.

What does impossible look like to you? Go ahead. Name it.

Restoration of your marriage?

A prodigal child or grandchild coming home?

Forgiven debt?

Healing of unresolved anger?

Freedom from addiction?

Life in service on a mission field?
Your country church doubling in size?
Come on. Think big. Pray deep.
God can do anything. Anything beyond what you can possibly imagine. And he wants to do it. For your good and his glory. He wants to give you a story you cannot keep silent. Because he loves you and me with a lavish sort of love.
That's what he was about to do for me.
Dare to dare. Ask.
Ask for Better Than Ever.

Lord, I pray that you will make my situation better than it has ever been before. Don't let me be content with the status quo any longer. Open my eyes to your world of boundless possibilities.

SEEING WITH FRESH EYES

What Better Than Ever have you hesitated to ask God for? Write it out and dare to ask.

5

Green Lights

Now to him who is able to do immeasurably
more than all we ask or imagine, according to his
power that is at work within us, to him be glory
in the church and in Christ Jesus throughout all
generations, for ever and ever! Amen.
—EPHESIANS 3:20–21

Iridescent green lights and flickering shadows played tag within my field of vision. Fluctuating pressure pressed against my left eye. Conversation in the surgical unit wove around the doctor's scheduled golf game, his request for a bigger tip for the ultrasonic drill, and the surgical tech's occasional check-in with me, asking if I was all right.

I was long past all right. I had moved into the zone of repeating Bible verses and praying for other people so I could block out the sensory and emotional overload of the surgical room. I tried not to think about why the surgery was taking so long, whether the surgery would even restore my fragile vision, and those ever-present green lights. What were they for anyway? The doctor's work lamp? Laser beams? I didn't know, and I didn't care. I just knew they were bright and annoying.

Although I didn't receive general anesthesia, the pre-op nurse said

I would be given a twilight sleep and probably remember nothing. I was aware of everything. I felt no pain but had to swallow the distasteful awareness of someone messing with my eye. A friend, who once worked as a surgical tech, had explained to me that retinal surgery is often done under local anesthesia because general anesthesia causes a higher risk of vomiting, which puts too much strain on the postsurgical eye. I understood that, but I didn't have to like it.

In hindsight, I'm glad I was awake. If I had been unconscious, I would have missed the doctor's words near the end of the surgery. "Mrs. Wingate, I'm usually cautious about making predictions, but I believe I can guarantee *your vision will be better than it has ever been before.*"

Had I heard correctly? My mind flitted to the prayer circle from the night before. Hadn't Fergy prayed those Better Than Ever words less than eighteen hours ago?

I knew Dr. Reddy would only say something like that if it were true. After all, this was the man who openly warned me that I might come out of surgery with no change or even worse vision. No one knew better than I the extent of the damage to both of my eyes. Those childhood surgeries had left a debris field of cataract fragments. The type of surgery used in the 1960s to address congenital cataracts had narrowed the pupil opening so tightly that my eyes were nearly impossible to dilate. Dr. Reddy had taken the opportunity during that retina surgery to clear out the debris field and widen the pupil to allow more light to hit the optic nerve. That is why he felt confident in saying those wonderful Better Than Ever words.

Despite low vision, God had given me all I needed. I could fill pages with stories of how God provided me transportation to travel all over the country even though I don't drive. A Bible seminary that didn't have services for disabled students recruited undergrads to read textbooks to me. At every point when work and my poor eyesight collided, computer technology took a leap forward, relieving the strain of seeing. I had an education, a family, a career, and a good ministry. God had answered my childhood prayer to help me live my life despite poor eyesight. I had learned to be content and grateful for the vision I did have.

And now this. Better Than Ever.

Miracles do happen. They aren't reserved for Bible heroes or missionaries in underdeveloped countries. They can happen to ordinary people like you and me. They happen when we pray or maybe when we don't pray. They'll happen regardless of how much faith we have; remember, I was the woman who said, "This can't happen." Miracles provide the chance to tell a story that invites other eyes to see all that God can do, ears to hear what else God has to say, and hearts to turn back toward God.

Miracles happen to show us that only God could do what has been done, that he alone is God, and there is nothing and no one else worthy of our worship.

And so I lay on that surgical gurney and worshipped a God who would, after fifty years, give sight to a blind woman.

I could relate to King David's reaction when the prophet Nathan told him his son would build the temple to the Lord and that David's line of descendants would reign forever: David was overwhelmed with worship. He sat before the Lord and said, "Who am I, Sovereign LORD, and what is my family, that you have brought me this far?" (2 Sam. 7:18).

> Each blessing gives a glimpse of God's generous, compassionate nature and his willingness to make you, ordinary you, a part of his bigger plan.

God blesses you every day in so many ways—and then pours on more. Each blessing gives a glimpse of God's generous, compassionate nature and his willingness to make you, ordinary you, a part of his bigger plan.

What blessings has God given you? Fill a page, a notebook. Buy another notebook for later. God is not done blessing you yet.

Is your mind as blank as the page before you? Ask God to show you how he works and, yes, how he loves. When he floods your mind and life with examples, worship him as the living God and get yourself ready to tell the story of what he has done for you.

Oh, Lord God, you can do anything. I can't even
begin to imagine what you can do. Show me in
my life or by watching the life of another what you
alone can do.

SEEING WITH FRESH EYES

What have you seen God do in your life or in another's life? Pause to worship him for that specific event. Tell God there is no one else like him.

6
Daydreams

Call to me and I will answer you and tell you great
and unsearchable things you do not know.
—JEREMIAH 33:3

$\mathcal{I}$magine someone promised that you would soon receive the best gift of your life, but then told you that you had to stay perfectly still for the next twenty minutes. That's what happened after that magical moment when the surgeon told me of Better Than Ever. We were in the middle of surgery, after all. I had to lie still and be quiet when I wanted nothing more than to dance and shout. Not fair! It was worse than hearing my mother tell me to stay in bed on Christmas morning.

Better Than Ever. I couldn't even imagine. Remember, this wasn't a restoration of health like so many surgeries accomplish. This was a first-time, never experienced before event. I had no clue what normally sighted people saw and I still don't. Just as you probably can't imagine how someone functions with only one eye, I cannot comprehend how two eyes possibly work together. And it blows my mind every time my husband reads a fast-food menu from across a room or why anyone thinks name tags are a necessary thing at conferences.

What would I be able to see?

How much better would Better Than Ever be?

What life tasks would be easier to do?

Driving would probably still be out of the question, but what else would I be able to do that I wasn't too old to try? Shoot baskets? Ride a bike? Climb mountains?

I lay on the surgical gurney, so amazed that the thing I had not allowed myself to dream of was actually happening. Where to start? What would I notice first?

Anticipation is sweet. Half the fun of the destination is dreaming about it. We've all had promises of wonderful upcoming events.

Graduation.

Marriage.

A once-in-a-lifetime vacation.

The birth of the first grandchild.

The job we've always wanted.

Hesitation mars our eagerness. We really want what we've always wanted, but now that it is here, what modifications will we need to make? Will we be able to adapt? I could have dealt with diminishing vision; I would have used the same coping skills I'd honed all my life. But I didn't know how to adjust to better vision. Was I too old to make those changes? Would my aging brain and atrophied optic nerve comprehend the new details my eyes could see? Oh, but wouldn't it be nice to try! Was there such a thing as physical therapy classes for the newly sighted?

We also fear that if we hope too much, the whims of fate will whisk our treasured dream from us. Maybe the doctor was being overconfident. Maybe I shouldn't hope too much.

Then I remembered what else happened the day of my mammogram. As I struggled with the realization that I might have to curtail my life activities if I had both loss of vision and breast cancer, I had the distinct impression that someone else was in the room, so enveloping that the space seemed small and claustrophobic. Then one sentence sounded in my mind, as clear as if someone had spoken out loud: *I am not done with you yet.*

It was God's promise to me. At the time, I took it to mean that God could and would use me in glorious ways even if I lost my health and vision. But the blessing of improved vision was what he had in mind. He knew my future. He knew he was about to give me Better Than Ever.

The God who had walked with me in the darkness would stay with me as I journeyed toward the light.

I had no clue that day, as I lay waiting for surgery to finish, what Better Than Ever would look like or the spiritual truths God would show me as I saw parts of his creation in my corner of the world for the very first time. But I did know that the God who had walked with me in the darkness would stay with me as I journeyed toward the light. He was expert at guiding me through the moments I both loved and feared. He had protected and cared for me and my family in ways we could not do ourselves.

If God has guided, provided, and protected us in the past, hasn't he proven himself reliable to do so in the future?

God had good reason to tell many Bible characters not to be afraid or discouraged about upcoming change. Life was tough at the moment, but he had something absolutely wonderful waiting for each of them. God never changes. He who walked with those men and women of faith and has walked with you in the past is the same God who will continue to walk with you in your future. He knows already how he plans to use your life from this point on to shout his glory. And, my friend, the moments he has waiting for you are so wonderful.

Hang on. God can do things with your life you never dreamed possible. It might be scary exciting, or it might just be scary. But through the process, he will reveal insights about his character and creation that you've never thought about before.

Because Better Than Ever is like entering a whole new world.

*Show me, Lord, what Better Than Ever you have
planned for me. Help me adapt so I can get the
most out of what you have planned for me.*

SEEING WITH FRESH EYES

What's your next adventure? Open the eyes of your imagination and daydream a bit about the possibilities. God is ready to go with you and show you things you never thought could happen.

7

The Floor

*Now faith is confidence in what we hope for and
assurance about what we do not see.*
—HEBREWS 11:1

The wait is worth it.

For two weeks after surgery, I had to lie face down, not doing anything, so the gas bubble that held everything in place inside my eye would not slip and the retinal tear could seal. As my back muscles tightened in protest and hours lengthened into days, I kept telling myself, "One day, I will see Better Than Ever."

"You've had limited vision all your life," one friend responded to my whine about the wait. "What's a few more weeks?"

The floor loomed large and I stared at nothing but the silver mesh of an eye guard. *Because,* I wanted to tell her, *I didn't have the promise before.* Promises breathe hope. Hope gives structure to a wait time and turns the unknown into the known. Seeing that something is possible and probable makes us want it even more.

I settled my face into my doughnut-shaped pillow. Waiting in hope was supposedly better than having no hope at all. In those long days,

it was small consolation. How could I possibly lie still when I wanted
to experience my new season of life?

Looking at the floor for two weeks was my darkest hour. "You'll be
better, but recovery takes time," health-care professionals told me. It's
the song everyone hears after surgery. Life must get worse before it gets
better. But it will get better.

Was clinging to hope during the hard moments the secret of those
dear saints of God whose portraits line the hall of faith in Hebrews 11?
Abraham had to go through the agonizing prospect of sacrificing his
son before he realized the permanence of God's promise to bless him
and his descendants (vv. 17–19). The Israelites had seven uncertain
days of marching around an enemy city before God brought down the
walls of Jericho (v. 30). The prostitute Rahab, who hid two Israelite
spies before the Jericho conquest, clung to their promise of deliverance in the form of a red cord they had given her to hang in her window. She must have stared at that promise-infused red cord day after
day, not knowing when her freedom would come, yet faith told her it
would come (v. 31).

A few Old Testament characters saw glimpses of God's promises.
Others saw nothing at all during their lifetime. "There were others
who were tortured, refusing to be released so that they might gain an
even better resurrection" (v. 35). These unnamed people of faith ended
their time on earth before God fulfilled his promises through Jesus.

I couldn't despair. I couldn't give up. I had something glorious waiting for me—Better Than Ever vision. So I spent my days imagining
what it would be like to live in light. I concocted a mental list of all
the things I wanted to see for the first time: a flowing waterfall, the
grandeur of a mountain, and the stones of my wedding ring.

I discovered later that I was wrong on so many counts about what
Better Than Ever would look like. But the imagining helped me endure, and as I lay in darkness, hope moved me toward the light. I
never doubted for a moment the reality of the promise. Someday. Better Than Ever.

But there was a catch to receiving the promise. "Do everything you are told to do and you will have better vision," the medical staff had said. So I followed their orders by lying still. And dreaming of glorious light.

Do you doubt there is such a thing as a Better Than Ever life? Yes, it happened to me, but perhaps you aren't so sure it will happen for you. An unmarred life without the weight of emotional baggage. Peace, goodwill, and restored relationships. It sounds wonderful, but do you have reason to hope?

Yes! The light of heaven beckons you home. The promise awaits. This life, this earthly dwelling, won't last forever. Life, in fact, may get worse before it gets better, but life eternal will be better than life has ever been before. As with those unnamed men and women of faith in Hebrews, God may not fix our immediate circumstances, but we can know for sure that eternity will be the best of any earthly Better Than Ever.

You and I have only a few clues of what eternity will look like. We don't know when it will happen to us, but our faith gives us confident hope that it will happen. And when we get there, we'll get it wrong on so many counts.

Endurance in the midst of the struggle is a form of righteous obedience.

While we wait, our challenge is to patiently endure the bad, the worse, and the unknown, because endurance in the midst of the struggle is a form of righteous obedience. I don't know about you, but it's enduring the here and now that is the tough part for me. It's much more difficult to obey God when life throws rocks at me or the dark keeps me from seeing where I'm going. Think of it this way, though. It's easier to obey when you know you have something great and glorious waiting for you on the other side.

So hang in there. Do all God has told you to do. On the days when it's extra tough, dream of heaven. Envision the open arms of your Savior, welcoming you home. And keep moving forward.

It's the hope that helps us endure the wait for the when.

Father, I wait in expectant hope for the when of
your promise. Even in the darkest gloom, I'll press
forward, trusting you will keep your part of the
promise as I follow you in faith.

SEEING WITH FRESH EYES

Create a list of what you are looking forward to about heaven.

8

Potato Salad

*Before they call I will answer; while they are still
speaking I will hear.*
—ISAIAH 65:24

*L*ying on my tummy, blind in one eye and unseeing in the other,
made me dependent on everyone for everything, even trips from
the couch to the bathroom. I couldn't be left alone unless I promised
not to move.

That meant I couldn't prepare meals. My husband has a list of four
meals he can fix: steak, steak, steak, and hamburgers. On a good day.
We were at the good-hearted mercy of church ladies for our meals. For
a type A kitchen control freak like me, you might as well put me on
death row. And asking for something special for myself is not part of
my genetic makeup. *Be cooperative and grateful for anything anyone does
for you*, my set jaw told me.

Who feels cooperative after any kind of surgery? It's acceptable to
be picky about creature comforts when you don't feel good, right? And
in all those hours of waiting to feel better, I distracted my mind with
any number of fantasies. Including food.

The ladies from my church fellowship truly were considerate. They stocked our refrigerator with small sandwiches, tortilla roll-ups, and other finger food I could pick up without seeing. One friend, thinking I'd have a tough time drinking coffee upside down, mailed chocolate-covered coffee beans. Any of my sweet friends would have jumped to meet my special requests.

I kept silent. Because that's the way I am. Or that's the way I thought I should be. But the one who knows me best peeked into my sluggish brain and tattled to the church ladies.

Some raspberry Jell-O made with applesauce would taste wonderful. That evening, Fergy delivered dinner, including applesauce-infused raspberry Jell-O. Had I told Fergy that was my favorite way to fix Jell-O?

The next day, visions of homemade macaroni and cheese sifted through my weary brain. Amy's dinner delivery was a big pan of macaroni and cheese.

This was no longer coincidence. I was scared to think anything.

But Saturday of that week, without mentioning my crazy cravings, I dared to think about potato salad. You guessed it. Sunday morning, Gloria brought lunch to our door before church. Potato salad was on the menu.

Isn't it beautiful? God knows our needs before we ask. He knows our wants and whims even when we don't ask.

God promised to walk the journey with us. He will not leave us or forsake us.

Answered prayer is more than God resolving the hard moments; it's learning to see God in the moment. Perhaps we need to pray more: *Lord, will you take care of me while I go through this?* He promised he would. God promised to walk the journey with us. He will not leave us or forsake us (Heb. 13:5). He will be with us (Isa. 41:10). He will take care of us (1 Peter 5:7) and provide for us as we journey toward the unknown. And he'll tuck in a few extra blessings because it gives us pleasure and it gives him delight to do so. It's his way of letting us know he is there, he loves us, and he will provide what we need to make it through the struggle. His mercy softens the harshness of the trial.

No, I didn't need my favorite Jell-O, homemade macaroni and cheese, or potato salad. But I did need the warm, soft embrace of my Abba Father's love and his feathered whisper on my ear: *I'm here, beloved daughter. I know everything that is happening to you. Put me in charge, and we'll get through this together.*

Try this during your next tough time. Pray for the vision to see how God shows up in the small moments. Ask for his sustaining strength and grace. Then get ready to be surprised. God loves you and delights in you. He knows what enters and exits your mind when no one else does. He loves to give you the desires of your heart and to show you that it comes from him.

Even potato salad.

Thank you, Lord God, for loving me so intimately that you provide the little things I like. Thank you for taking such good care of me.

SEEING WITH FRESH EYES

Reflect on the last few days. What unexpected gifts has God given you? How have you sensed that he has been with you during your everyday moments?

9

God Glimpses

Come and see what God has done, his awesome
deeds for mankind!
—PSALM 66:5

I was ready to see. I lifted my face from my doughnut pillow, pre-pared to claim the promise. But my dominant eye, weakened by inflammation, unused to the glare caused by a widened pupil, and blurred by a now obsolete lens refraction, refused to cooperate. One morning, I curled into a fetal position, resisting the temptation to cry tears of frustration because the salted moisture would aggravate my reddened eye.

Do you get the idea that patience is not one of my spiritual gifts? Give me a break. That specialist said I was going to see Better Than Ever. Who wanted to wait one moment longer? And yet, the gift of sight sat like a birthday package, tied with a gilt ribbon, and tagged with the words *Do not open until . . .* when?

God, I cried, *I want to see now. Why must you take so long to let me have this gift you've promised?*

In the periphery of my daily life, I became aware that God was showing up in other ways. The gifts of my favorite food were only the opening scenes of a month-long premiere of his goodness. So I turned my back on blurred images of my long-term and resolved to look for God in the close-up of my everyday ordinary.

"It's her mind that will do her seeing for her," my childhood surgeon had said so many years ago. Was that true in the spiritual realm as well? Would I see God at work more clearly if I intentionally looked for him? "Seek and you will find," the Bible says (Matt. 7:7). Would that, could that, happen? I prayed that God would part the curtain and give me a behind-the-scenes tour of how he was working everything for my good, as another Bible verse, Romans 8:28, promised.

Each morning, God presented me the gift of continued healing and renewed strength to cope with my distorted eyesight. I leaned in closer to see what he was doing. I was amazed. He was at work for my benefit. I just had not noticed. Day after day, I caught glimpses of his glory all around me.

A mistake on our hospital bill reduced our payment by over half. My useless right eye rose to the challenge and ushered in enough vision for me to navigate through my house and to the mailbox on my own. The only clear sight in my left eye was my midrange vision, the perfect distance to see my computer screen. This allowed me to meet writing deadlines, journal my journey to better sight, and chat with four Facebook friends who had recently found out they too needed retinal surgery.

"Isn't God good?" one church friend said.

Open the eyes of your heart and mind to see the small things.

Yes, he is. Like lightning surrounding a desert city during a storm, illuminating majestic mountain peaks, glimpses of God's glory flash around our daily lives, showing off what he has been up to. If we want to enjoy the light show, we must step outside and watch. We train ourselves to track the trail of the storm so we can see where the lightning strikes. We can't see everything God is doing at the moment, but in his mercy, he lets us see enough to gain new confidence in his existence and his concern for our best.

Where is God working right now in your life? Instead of despairing at his apparent silence or absence, open the eyes of your heart and mind to see the small things. Ask him to show you what he is doing today. Thank him for being part of your everyday while you wait in hopeful expectation for the grand reveal of his glory.

How can you notice what God is doing? Pretend you are on a scavenger hunt. At the start of each day, invite the Lord to be your tour guide. Ask him to point out the telltale signs of his presence tucked into the nooks and crannies of your life. When you see what he sees, you'll be impressed with the incredible detail of his miraculous creativity. You'll discover that instead of abandoning you, he has plans to share with you so much more than you could possibly imagine.

Lord, come with me this day. Help me find you and
your work within my ordinary moments.

SEEING WITH FRESH EYES

Keep a notepad near you during the next twenty-four hours. Record every time you see God working specifically on your behalf, whether providing for your needs or working out details so you can serve him better.

PART 2

. . . HAVE SEEN A GREAT LIGHT

10

Bathroom Scales

Come, let us bow down in worship, let us kneel
before the LORD our Maker.
—PSALM 95:6

One month had passed since my retina specialist uttered those hope-filled, Better Than Ever words. Curious what recovery inactivity had done to my weight, I wandered into the bathroom and stepped on the scale.

With my eye still healing and my visual acuity changing daily, I doubted I could see the scale's numbers from any distance. Determined not to have my husband read the numbers to me, I started to do what I've done all my life. I bent over as far as my flabby body allowed and prepared to guess on the low side of the readout.

Blurred digits stared at me, causing me to jerk upright. The blur turned into a crisp, well-defined readout. I could read the number from a standing position. I had never read the numbers, ever, from a standing position. But this morning, I could.

The battery's lifetime guarantee was in dire jeopardy as I stepped off and back on five times. I don't even remember what I weighed. The joy of seeing trumped the reality of what I saw. It was happening. The day of first discovery had come.

Tears filled my eyes. I could have never anticipated this side effect of better vision. Reading the scale was a long-held private frustration. What woman wants to ask someone else to read the numbers for her? And yet, like any red-blooded female, I wanted to know. Never again would I have to bend or kneel on the scale so I could see the numbers.

It was real. The doctor was right. I would see Better Than Ever. I must have gained two pounds from the joy flowing into my soul. *Oh, thank you, Jesus. I can see!*

Clutching my robe, I ran through the house, shouting the good news to Jack. Then I headed to my computer to share my excitement on Facebook with those beautiful people who had prayed for this moment.

Reactions from my friends set me back.

"Praise God—I guess," one friend commented. "Couldn't you find something else to be the first?" another wrote. "God sure has a sense of humor," a third said. Their point was clearer than the tip of an analog needle. Bathroom scale readouts were nice and practical—but couldn't my first sight discovery have been something beautiful and impressive, something worthy of the telling?

God grabs our attention in the unexpected moments, leaving no doubt about the origin of the gift.

God grabs our attention in the unexpected moments, leaving no doubt about the origin of the gift. Imagine if the first new thing I saw had been leaves on trees, flower petals, or rain-laden clouds. That's what everyone expected. And they would have scrolled on to the next Facebook entry.

The glory of what God had done would have been lost. But the bathroom scale piqued my friends' curiosity. It made us all pause. Wonder. Think. Praise.

Angels announced the birth of Christ to shepherds first rather than to kings and emissaries. A visit from heavenly beings to lowlifes like them caught everyone's attention. The unusual choice made generations to come notice and remember. And then the unconventional baby bed—a feeding trough—validated the angel's message. Yes. This is the one. The unexpected marked the miraculous.

Mary Magdalene was the first to see Jesus after he came back to life. Jesus could have chosen one of the apostles, Nicodemus, Pilate, his mother, or a Jerusalem crowd out for a Sunday stroll. No, God chose a formerly demon-possessed woman to be his public relations spokesperson. Mary's testimony propelled Peter and John toward the tomb to see if these things were so. The unexpected became a call to action.

Like Mary's reunion with the resurrected Jesus in the garden, my first encounter of new sight was private and personal. The God who knows me inside and out, who created every fiber of my being, and who is not ashamed of my nakedness desired that this moment of firstfruits discovery be reserved for him and him alone.

If I'd been with other people and seen some outside wonder we'd expected to be my first, my exclamation of surprised delight would have drawn attention to me and what I was looking at. Instead, God chose a private setting to unwrap the gift of my new vision so I could share the joy first with the Giver of the gift. Just God and me, by ourselves, delighting over the gift together. I think I could even sense his delighted chuckle. I stood in wonder and worship of a God who loved me so much that he thought about my frustration over reading numbers on a bathroom scale.

What unexpected thing has God done for you? Thank him first. Alone. Then proclaim the good news to anyone ready to listen: *I have seen the Lord.*

Lord, help me see your unexpected touches in the private rooms of my routine. As I see you at work, I

want to share those moments of celebration with
you first.

SEEING WITH FRESH EYES

Name something specific God has done for you in the last few days.
Pause and tell him thank you for what he has done.

11

Dirt

For you created my inmost being; you knit me
together in my mother's womb.
—PSALM 139:13

Not much of a gardener, I'm usually able to stash some petunias, begonias, or geraniums in the planter in front of my house by Mother's Day. This year was different. Nearby yards flourished with colorful blooms, but my garden lay barren.

After the doctor's orders released me to resume life at my choice of speed, I ventured outside with oversize sunglasses, still blinking against the glare. Eager to do something, anything, that wouldn't challenge my surgery-sensitive eyes, I surveyed my desolate yard.

That's when I saw dirt.

Before my surgery, dirt had been nothing more than a homogenous smudge under my moving feet. Now I could see what everyone else saw—the texture and topography of dirt.

My farmer friends wanted to correct me when I told them the story. It's soil, not dirt, they said. Whatever they wanted to call it, I saw it, and it was beautiful and exciting. For the first time in my life, I saw a myriad of particles that support plant life. With the fascination of a four-year-old, I let a fistful of dark brown dirt sift from one hand to the other like a slow-moving Slinky.

God refuses to be a functional God. He could have whipped up one recipe of potting soil, spread it over all the earth's land surfaces, and called it good. Instead, he splashed dirt with multimillion variety, inventing beauty by its breadth of creativity. There's the dark, rich soil of the Midwest, the red clay of Georgia, and the sandy beach of Florida's oceanfront. The Creator wasn't bothered about the needed tonnage to cover landmasses; in his divine mind, more variations showcased his infinite ingenuity.

Dirt deserves the same awe and wonder we reserve for majestic waterfalls and monarch butterflies. In a farmer's mind, there is nothing more beautiful than a well-turned field, ready for planting. Dirt is rich with nutrients and composted matter, yet interrelated to the rest of nature in its dependence on moisture and temperature to sustain life. It becomes a habitat for all kinds of critters—life-forms that give back to the earth through their decaying bodies. Dirt holds the earth together. It is as basic to our existence as the bread on our tables. Without it, we would have no food supply, no oxygen to breathe, no firm place to stand.

In God's economy, scarcity does not make a thing more valuable.

The law of supply and demand might apply to a capitalistic society, but it doesn't work in God's marketplace. In God's economy, scarcity does not make a thing more valuable. God must have liked dirt so much that he made a lot of it. Then, like an overeager scientist, he played with the formula, concocting and constructing it to fit the unique needs of each ecosystem.

So much dirt, but every acre so different from the rest. And the deeper you look, the more detail you see. Pausing to ponder strips away the ubiquity and reveals the diversity.

Just like people.

Some sociologists estimate that a hundred billion people have populated the earth, each of them connected to the dust of the ground from which God made the first man (Gen. 2:7). Think of it. Such a large number would hint that human life is cheap, too common to be of much worth. Yet God values each person. Every individual is beautiful and precious in God's sight. He lavishes his love on each of us, customizing us with the same intricacy and variation he used when he made dirt. Just as dirt is plentiful, unique, complex, and an essential, foundational part of earthly creation, so the life of the human race is as well.

Human life as common as dirt? Yes—common and complicated, valuable and valued.

Go ahead. Step outside. Grab a handful of dirt. Let it filter through your fingers and collect beneath your nails. Sort through the wealth of detail. Count the shades of brown. Feel the difference between hard pebbles and slimy mud. Breathe deep and let the dust make you sneeze, then inhale the scent again after a summer's rain.

After each sensation, thank God for the artistry and time he put into the creation of the earth. Then go hug the human being next to you, grateful that God chose to make that person as precious, beautiful, customized, unique, and purpose-filled as dirt.

Wash your hands first. Or not.

Thank you, God, for making me wonderfully one of a kind. Thank you for making the person next to me equally complex, yet different. Your creativity is amazing.

SEEING WITH FRESH EYES

Choose the person in your circle of acquaintances who is most different from you. List five things you share in common with that person. Number one on your list could be, "God made both of us."

12

Color

*For he has rescued us from the dominion of
darkness and brought us into the kingdom of the
Son he loves, in whom we have redemption, the
forgiveness of sins.*
—COLOSSIANS 1:13–14

*E*asing back into the normal paces of home life, I tackled piles of laundry for the first time since my surgery. Pulling clothes from the dryer, my hand stilled. One blouse had lost its familiar look. The color was off: it seemed brighter, maybe more intense. Not the pink softened by years of wear that I remembered. The truth brought my hand to life as I crumpled the warm, fresh-scented, fiercely fuchsia cloth in my fingers and held it against my face.

The blouse had not changed. My vision had.

For weeks, I'd wondered what my retina specialist meant by "better vision." Would objects appear bigger, more detailed, or less blurry? No on bigger. Dirt told me yes on the boundless level of detail. The bathroom scales shouted new clarity.

I hadn't counted on color brilliance.

Color is a by-product of light, a children's science book told me.

Color allows us to discriminate between objects, the dictionary said. Color is bent light. The more light, the brighter the color.

Dim light strips color and blurs clarity. Imagine a world without color. Defined only by its shape and mass, everything would otherwise look the same.

Before Better Than Ever, my ability to see shape and detail was limited, so color used to be my go-to method of distinguishing what I saw. "Don't ever change your color," I told a red-haired friend. "That's how I know who you are."

I thought I saw color like everyone else because it was the one strong visual attribute I had. Now, as I stared at the blouse in my hands, I realized how wrong I was. I shouldn't have been surprised. The widening of my surgically stuck pupil allowed more light to strike the optic nerve, and with light came color brilliance.

> The closer we move toward the light of Jesus, the more distinctive and alluring our character will become.

Jesus has brought us out of darkness into the light of his love, purity, and goodness. When we stand in his presence, we reflect that light. Remember? Light draws out and heightens color. Observers of our lives will see the brilliant brightness our lives reflect, which stands in stark contrast to the drab gray of their dim environment. How much of a contrast will depend on how close we stand to Jesus. The closer we move toward the light of Jesus, the more distinctive and alluring our character will become. We'll be as eye-catching as a dazzling leading lady under a spotlight on an otherwise darkened stage.

Perhaps that's why Paul encouraged the Colossian Christians to clothe themselves with a rainbow spectrum of attributes that would make them look like Jesus: compassion, kindness, humility, gentleness, patience, forbearance, forgiveness, and love (Col. 3:12–14). Those are the colors of our character that will help others recognize that we've been with Jesus. He wants our character to shine brightly enough that others notice and give glory to God (Matt. 5:16). This is what will happen, for Jesus's light makes a life committed to him as radiant as the brightest of rainbows.

If you want your relationship with Christ to color your character, start by moving closer to Jesus. That means spending time with him, doing life his way instead of following your own desires, and obeying his directives even when it is not convenient to do so.

As you grow in your relationship with him, you'll become more beautiful and radiant. You'll glow with that inner light that comes only from Jesus. Your more vivid and visible faith will attract family, friends, and strangers to the delightful life Jesus has to offer. They'll ask questions and long to have what you have and be clothed with the beautiful characteristics you wear.

It's okay. Step into his light. Let Jesus color your world.

Shine on me, Lord, so I will reflect all the beauty of your character in a way that others will notice and want what you have to offer.

SEEING WITH FRESH EYES

Choose one of the character traits from Colossians 3:12–14 that is difficult for you to portray. Do a Bible word search and read what the Bible says about that trait, asking God to help you shine more brightly in that area.

13

Clocks

*Because of the L<small>ORD</small>'s great love we are not
consumed, for his compassions never fail. They are
new every morning; great is your faithfulness.*
—LAMENTATIONS 3:22–23

*I*n the days before smartphones, nightstand clocks were my nemesis. We have gone through several alarm clocks in our years of marriage, trying to find one I could see. For middle of the night awakenings, a talking clock was not an option.

One day, an online catalog advertised a clock that projected the time and temperature on the ceiling. It was the kind of whiz-bang gift my husband would like, I might see the large projected numbers, and we would both enjoy knowing the morning temperature first thing. It would be a perfect gift for my typically hard-to-please man. His birthday was long past, but I bought it anyway, telling him it was my birthday gift to myself because, well, I hoped I had found a clock I could read.

He loved it and set it up immediately. We lay on the bed together, staring at the ceiling.

"Can you see it?"

"Well . . ." I couldn't. "It's the middle of the day. Let's try again after dark."

Night came. All I saw was a brown tinge. I got pouty. "Happy early birthday," I grumbled. "It's all yours."

Reading clock numbers didn't rank on the bucket list of things I wanted to see after Better Than Ever. I didn't even think about the projection clock. But several months after Better Than Ever, I woke to a quiet house. Baxter, our Welsh corgi, made sleepy sounds in his cage, and my beloved husband snored beside me. A bright red blur glowed above my head.

I wonder . . .

I plucked my glasses from the nightstand. 6:45 a.m. 65 degrees. I could even read the *F* for Fahrenheit. My dear one stirred, and I grabbed his hand, forgetting that people turn in bed while still asleep. "Hey, you, I can read the clock."

Fully awake, catching the significance of what I said, he rolled over, telling me to read what I saw. We lay there for five minutes with me reading the numbers every time they changed. He chuckled and I cried.

Every morning now, the first thing I see when I open my eyes are those red numbers, and I remember what God did for me. Every morning, I exhale and whisper, *Oh, thank you, God, for eyes to see clock numbers.* It's become a ritual to snuggle in the warmth of early morning blankets and revel in the miracle.

My red glow has become a kind of memorial, like what Joshua, Moses's successor, gave to the Israelites. After God's people crossed the Jordan River on dry ground—at flood stage, no less—Joshua ordered the priests to set up memorial stones. When their children and later generations would ask them the meaning of the stones, the people were to tell the story of God's rescue and redemption (Josh. 4:1–9).

My gratitude for every-morning eyesight was spontaneous and heartfelt. But I possessed other lifetime gifts that deserved equally delighted praise. I got a red glow of another idea. What have I always had for which I could thank God each morning?

A lone dove call sounded over the air conditioner's hum. *Thank you, God, that I can hear.*

Blanket fuzzies surrounded my early morning with warmth. *Thank you that I own a blanket.*

Baxter turned in his crate and sighed. *Thank you for a dog's companionship and energetic goofiness that makes me smile first thing and get moving right away.*

My mind turned toward the day's plans. *Thank you for today's anticipated activities.* What would I fix for breakfast? *Thank you for food in our fridge and strength in my hands to prepare meals.*

Jack let out an extra loud snort. *Thank you for this dear one who speaks your truth in the pulpit and within our home with eloquence.*

Each morning turned into praise points for what I had instead of a litany of wishes for what I didn't have.

What might prompt you to praise God first thing in the morning?

What might prompt you to praise God first thing in the morning? What can act as your morning trumpet call to worship? Have you almost lost the one beside you? Let those soft, sleepy sounds remind you of God's awesome work of mercy. Did you receive the possessions strewn about you in ways that speak of God's special provision? Use the sight of them to thank the Giver.

You'll find something worth mentioning to God, for the whole earth is filled with God's wonders. Psalm 65:8 says, "Where morning dawns, where evening fades, you call forth songs of joy." The item that calls forth your song of joy can become the first of many gratitude prompts that describe God's lavish love, never-ending faithfulness, and incredible goodness.

What a way to start the day.

Lord, I want to keep my eyes open to all you've
given me and done for me. May your Holy Spirit
reveal the signs of your faithfulness each morning
so I can praise you once again.

SEEING WITH FRESH EYES

Determine to thank God tomorrow for the first thing you see when
you open your eyes. Then write it down for you to remember God's
mercy. Consider making this a daily practice.

14

Fireworks and Smoke

This is what the Sovereign LORD, the Holy One
of Israel, says: "In repentance and rest is your
salvation, in quietness and trust is your strength,
but you would have none of it."
—ISAIAH 30:15

$\mathcal{J}$t was the Fourth of July, and the show began as dusk eased toward dark. I could hardly wait. I love fireworks. I have always enjoyed watching the bright orbs of color fill the sky. What would I see now?

That night's display did not disappoint. Before Better Than Ever eyesight, I saw fuzzy meshes of color, their aftermath of light appearing as lines trailing toward the horizon. Now I saw a thousand sprinkles of light, brilliant shards of stained glass glistening against a twilight sky. It was spectacular.

The crowd of friends and neighbors thought so too. "Ooh." "Ahh." "Pretty." "I love that purple one."

Color faded and crowd noise reduced to ordinary chitchat.

"I see the smoke."

Conversation stopped. "What did she say?"

"She saw smoke."

"Who?"

"Karen. Karen can see the smoke."

Of course there is smoke after fireworks. Everyone knows that. Right? No. I didn't.

Fifteen heads lifted their eyes to the sky. And my friends realized the precious gift of being able to see smoke after fireworks. The wonder was in its subtle existence.

The Old Testament prophet Elijah expected spectacular results from God's light show. Calling King Ahab and his cronies to account for their crimes against the Almighty, Elijah gathered the people of Israel, including four hundred prophets of the false god Baal, to Mount Carmel. "Who is truly God?" he challenged them. "Let's see who shows up." It was a gutsy call, yet God delivered a sensational display of fire from heaven that confirmed his sole power and authority over creation.

It wasn't enough to change hearts, especially one heart. Queen Jezebel burned with fury and threatened Elijah's life. Elijah ran for the hills and hid in a cave, feeling abandoned and alone. "I am the only one left," he told God (1 Kings 19:10). *No one else in all of Israel serves the one true God besides me*, Elijah must have thought. Wind, earthquake, and fire mangled the mountains around him, but God was not in those powerful forces. Instead, God spoke using a gentle whisper to call Elijah to his next mission.

God whispers into every moment, whatever the hour or event. Yet, as human beings, we often look for him only in the loud and spectacular.

Powerful preaching.

Buoyant worship.

Breaking news of miraculous healing that catches everyone's attention.

Like the Pharisees of Jesus's day, we look for signs of God's power. We demand lavish displays and visible wonders that prove his existence, interest, love, and protection. We want instant healing, obvious rescue, and life-changing miracles that would be fodder for a blockbuster movie or reality show retelling.

God can and does work in marvelous, fire-exploding ways. He also speaks in wisps of smoke and silence, working quietly behind the scenes in ways we may miss if we aren't looking intently in his direction.

God moments occur in the hearts of listeners as they grapple with a message and choose to do something about it.

The spectacular doesn't happen at the point of powerful preaching. God moments occur in the hearts of listeners as they grapple with a message and choose to do something about it. The proof of God's power is not in the polished words of the speaker, but in the resulting conviction within the heart of the listener.

God would take care of Jezebel in his own way. *For now*, the still, small voice said, *your task, Elijah, is to do the next thing. Strengthen yourself, recruit your replacement, and appoint the next ring of world leaders.* (See 1 Kings 19:15–18.)

What do you want of God? Do you wish he would show himself to you? To others in your life who rebel against him? Do you want instant healing or dramatic conflict resolution that would prove he has the power and authority to do such things? Do you find yourself asking, *Where is God? Why won't he show himself?*

He is here. He is but a breath of faint smoke away, working in you to do the next thing. His quiet voice speaks into the silence with as much power as the shock and awe of the largest firestorm. His glory may not emblazon the sky, at least this time, but he is still there. His working for our good goes on—undeterred, not always noticeable, but still very present.

Quiet moments can come in many forms: a new understanding about thorny biblical concepts, an idea that pops into your head when you've prayed for wisdom on how to handle a relationship snag, a found key ring after hours of searching, the hoot of an owl on a calm summer's evening, or a card of encouragement arriving in the mail on the day you've reached your lowest point. God is in those occurrences as much as he is in what most would call the miraculous. Like pausing to look at an object under the lens of a microscope, it takes more time to find the finer details of God's power at work, but the quiet, consistent signs of his presence are no less spectacular.

Today, look for the small things. When random coincidences happen, ask yourself how God might have been in the making. When you pray for peace within your household and one volatile family member doesn't react as usual, make the connection. You prayed, didn't you? During those times that the rest of the world or other faith walkers call powerful, go deeper. Look for what else God is doing to make himself known and turn hearts toward him.

Those moments are there, waiting to be discovered. Like smoke after fireworks.

Forgive me, Lord, for the times I demand big,
visible displays of your power and goodness. I
commit myself to follow your small whispers of
instruction that lead me toward the next step of
your perfect plan.

SEEING WITH FRESH EYES

Go on a God hunt. The next time you gather with a group of believers, listen and watch. How do you observe God working among his people?

15

Window View

*I saw the Holy City, the new Jerusalem, coming
down out of heaven from God, prepared as a bride
beautifully dressed for her husband.*
—REVELATION 21:2

A Facebook friend posted a photo of the view outside his office window: palm trees silhouetted against a blazing sunrise with a backdrop of ocean waves off the east coast of Florida. I was jealous. I wanted pretty scenery outside my office window. If I got to see that amazing sight every day, I rationalized, I'd be far more productive and creative.

I'm forever scouring my neighborhood for pleasant places, pretty bits of scenery that will inspire me to greatness. I try out new coffee shops or hole up in hospital waiting rooms near bird aviaries while my preacher husband does afternoon visitations. But my home office holds all my resources, including my coffee maker and computer, and most of the time, I must be content with what I see from my window.

After pouting over pictures of palm trees, I peeked around my curtain at the view to the west, hoping for a glint of sunset glory. All I could see was the back door of the Nazarene church that shared our property line. My discontent returned.

Shame on me.

What could be more beautiful than a church building?

Beauty is found in both its expression and its interpretation. We consider something aesthetically pleasing if it is perfect in symmetry and design, unblemished, and pleasurable to our senses. But beauty is more than that. Our minds call it beautiful if we can connect a thing with pleasant memories or place it in the same category with other sites we've seen. Soil is beautiful to a farmer because it signifies the miracle of harvest. The bathroom scale will forever hold an element of beauty for me, for it tells of the moment I realized I could see better. Seven Falls in southern Arizona's Bear Canyon is as beautiful to me as Niagara Falls because of many happy hikes with my family during my childhood. It's a matter of perspective—the angle from which we view with the eyes of the heart.

Fine. But what's so beautiful about a church building?

Church buildings represent the assembly of the church—a global group of believers Christ established after his death and resurrection. The buildings symbolize God's choice to call together and use ordinary people to extend his gift of grace to those still caught in sin's mucky pit and re-create them into his perfection. The physical grandeur of stained glass windows is nothing compared to the portraits of unconditional love, unyielding faith, and unimaginable peace radiating from the faces of those gathered to worship their God. Simple buildings and grand cathedrals both hold the best of human life and the working together of many for one purpose. It's the best of beautiful.

You're kidding, right? The church—beautiful?

Mainstream media, the mouthpiece of worldly thinking, lures us to look at the flaws of the church. Anyone hurt by church dysfunction is tempted to put a magnifying lens on that sin, dismissing the church at large as unworthy, unpleasant, and ugly. Despite her flaws, the church community is still beautiful. The original design for this community of believers whom God ordained to carry his good news into the world is perfect because the Designer is perfect.

If you have trouble seeing beauty in the church next door, try this change of perspective. The church is not a completed entity; it is a work in progress. Rough-hewn beams of a building under construction foreshadow a structure of beauty, but it's not there yet. I can just imagine God lifting his head from his work at hearing a criticism about one of his flawed but beloved children and calling out from heaven, "Hold on, I'm not done yet."

The Church Beautiful is found in what it is and does, who it represents, and what it produces.

The Church Beautiful is found in what it is and does, who it represents, and what it produces. I see a group of people trying to reinvent their earthly lives by aligning themselves with God's original purposes for them. A community working together to do good in their corner of the world and showing those around them what God's grace looks like. I see gatherings where people celebrate their shared faith in many creative ways, everything from dinners to music, hobbies, life groups, and study sessions. I watch people living out what it means to sincerely love each other from the heart and worshipping God in the best way they know how with the limited resources they have.

Are they perfect at it? Not by a long shot. At times, those precious people are rather clumsy in their worship, fellowship, and treatment of each other. But, in their rough-hewn way, they are doing their best to honor the Lord they love and tell others about their good, good God.

Take a closer look at the house of worship you attend. Walk through its halls during a weekday. Look beyond the structure and imagine the activity that happens in each room that brings honor to God. Remember the happy moments you've spent in that building, the songs and speaking you've heard, the meals and good talks you've shared around its tables, and the times you've watched God work among his people.

Relive those worship services where you've felt called out of the chaos of the world to enter a place of peace and healing for your soul.

Remember what is beautiful about the church and combine your efforts with those of other Christ followers to honor God and be the best God has planned for all of you to be. For the beauty of the church is not found in its impressive architecture but in the life-giving message it has to share and the way it strives to represent the perfection of Jesus.

It's incredibly beautiful.

*Lord, at times I've been unhappy with
what I've seen in this collective group of people
you call the church. Show me today what is good
and beautiful about the community of believers
outside my window.*

SEEING WITH FRESH EYES

What makes the group of believers with whom you worship beautiful? If you don't currently have close connections with a church group, ask a local staff member or a longtime church member to share with you what makes that congregation beautiful to them.

16

King Tut

You know when I sit and when I rise; you perceive
my thoughts from afar.
—PSALM 139:2

I love museums and seek them out wherever I go. I own bragging rights to firsthand sights of Frank Borman's astronaut suit, a Kitty Hawk biplane replica with twin pusher props, and Pat Nixon's inaugural ball gown.

Okay. Truth: I saw shiny silver, white boards, and glittery yellow that other people told me were an astronaut suit, an airplane, and Pat Nixon's ball gown.

I'm not sure I can fully describe the wave of emotion I felt when I walked into a museum after Better Than Ever. For the first time in my life, I could act like a normal patron. *Normal,* by my definition, doesn't bend over barricades or ask family members to identify artifacts and read signs out loud. I could sit somewhere other than the front row in the theater. I didn't have to joke that I whiz through displays because I'm an ADD kind of museum visitor while inwardly my brain screamed to see and know. When others marvel at details of artifacts, I no longer need to pretend that I see them too.

Visiting any museum after Better Than Ever would have satisfied. That wasn't good enough for my God. He had a better idea, something he had been saving just for me for that very moment. Intent on light shows of his glory, he invited me to tour the exhibit I had longed to see for nearly four decades.

When I had the chance to visit Chicago's Field Museum as a seventeen-year-old, I got the mistaken idea that the King Tut exhibit would be on display. I was so excited. To my dismay, the exhibit had ended six months before. As a consolation prize, I bought a book in the museum gift shop that I kept for years, dreaming of the day I might yet see the famed display. As years rolled by, my dream waned, the book lay on a yard-sale table, and I forgot about young King Tut.

Three months after Better Than Ever, the King Tut exhibit came to a museum sixty miles from my home. "Do you want to go see it?" my girlfriends asked. Do April showers bring May flowers? Does the sun shine? *Yes!*

I'm glad I had to wait all those years. The exhibit was everything I had hoped for, even more. Artifacts and descriptions made more sense than they would have to a seventeen-year-old. Best of all, I saw more than blurry blobs and unreadable signs. I saw the intricate designs on replicas of the four shrines leading to King Tut's sarcophagus—the ancient stone coffin in which the Egyptian king was buried—and the detail on the death mask that covered the young king's head. I marveled at the artistry of the amulets filling a presentation case. And I could read as many placards as my brain could absorb.

Like the good, good Father he is, God chose to save the treasure of my desire for when my mind and my sight could fully appreciate it.

God didn't stop with a simple sight-renewal surgery. He packed a heaven-sized vault with visual wonders he wanted me to see when I was ready to see. The King Tut exhibit as my first museum visit was one more piece of evidence that each new wonder I saw was intentional and planned.

In those after-surgery days, lying facedown on my doughnut pillow, I spent hours concocting a list of what I wanted to see once Better Than

Ever began. God had already constructed his list, one far better than mine, representing what I wanted most. He remembered my struggles and longings. I would have never included things like bathroom scales, dirt, and a teenage girl's infatuation with Egyptian history. But God did, because he had a greater purpose. He caught my attention by giving me my heart's desire and then produced the life lesson he wanted me to hear.

After King Tut, I looked at what I saw each day with a new focus. Each new sighting was no longer happenstance but divinely intentional. Each had a purpose and fit into God's overall plan to fill my life with his lavish best, a plan devised long before the thought of better eyesight was on my mental radar.

He fulfills these kinds of wishes because he loves us. His rich gifts demonstrate that he knows everything in our minds, and like a loving Father, he takes pleasure in sharing. His grace is amazing.

> We don't need to work so hard for the fulfillment of our dreams. God is much better at choosing when and where to give us his best gifts.

We don't need to work so hard for the fulfillment of our dreams. God is much better at choosing when and where to give us his best gifts. If we find our delight in him and trust his best judgment, he will go above and beyond what we can ever begin to ask or imagine (see Eph. 3:20).

What's on God's dream list for you to see? All those things that happen in your life don't have to look like mere happenstance. When you put yourself under the lordship of Jesus, you allow yourself to come under the umbrella of his best plans for you. Life events are no longer "just the way things happen." Instead, ordinary moments intersect with God's plans and bigger picture for your life.

Isn't that exciting?

Here's an idea for you. We often ask God for his blessings on our plans. And then we become frustrated when our plans don't work out like we wanted. Instead, why not ask God to show you his plan book for you? *Lord, what do you want me to do?*

This doesn't mean you don't plan at all. It means you hold your plans loosely. When things don't turn out as you would like, you accept that that's part of God's plan. He is still working to bring all things together for good, and he can use even the snags, delays, and opposition to bring about his best for us.

He knows the plans he has for you, and they're going to be so good. In fact, they're going to be awesome.

Lord, in the wait for your answers to my deepest longing, I need to remember that you are making your gift to me extra lavish because you love me so much. I trust you to do your best for me.

SEEING WITH FRESH EYES

How has God provided for you in some unexpected, specific way? Thank him for knowing you so intimately and for caring so deeply about you.

17

Nothing

Ask and it will be given to you; seek and you will
find; knock and the door will be opened to you.
—MATTHEW 7:7

*A*fter the discovery of dirt, smoke, and bathroom scale numbers, I returned to my daily routine, playing catch-up on what I had let go during recovery. For several days, I noticed nothing different. The glow began to fade.

Why wasn't I seeing new things? Had I imagined the change? Would a few clods of dirt and color saturation be the extent of my miracle? Perhaps I was already taking new sight for granted, forgetting what it was like to not see. Had I moved into complacency, failing to wonder at the beauty of the seen?

The retina specialist said my vision would continue to improve for up to six months. My arm mimicked the movement of a trombone player as I bent it back and forth, constantly calculating how far from my face to hold anything to get a clear image. To make the situation more confusing, opticians ordered the wrong lens prescription, making it doubly hard to know what I was supposed to be able to see.

When I grumped about the never-ending adjustments, Jack

reminded me that refractions and adapting to new distances were external changes, easily solved with time, patience, and experimentation. The cure was real. Obstacles don't define change; they merely obscure it.

How like my faith walk.

Not so many years before, I stood on a plateau in my relationship with God. I attended church, read my Bible, taught Sunday school, and did service projects. I was secure in my level of faith, confident in my grasp of basic doctrine, and slightly arrogant about my righteous lifestyle. But something bugged me. The Bible I read told of ever-changing growth, leading us to become more like Jesus every day. I couldn't see any changes. I felt like I was stuck in the status quo. Was there more? What was I missing?

One squabble with my husband or one stress-laced day that made me pout over the unfairness of life proved I had a long way to go before I looked like Jesus. Doubt-filled questions arose. Did the Holy Spirit reside within me? Was this Jesus thing for real? Or was I deluding everyone about the faith-filled life while remaining empty inside?

Have you doubted your salvation? Wondered about the source of the problem—his reality or your faith?

You aren't alone. John the Baptist hit the snag of doubt too.

John rode a wave of popularity and success in his work of proclaiming the coming Messiah. Large crowds listened to him. He'd baptized Jesus and saw the Spirit descend upon his head. Then Herod slapped him in prison and John's work came to a screeching halt (Luke 3:19–20). As in the darkness of night when everything looks bad, John had hours of alone time to ponder, muse, and doubt. Was Jesus the Messiah, or should John and his disciples look for another? Finally, John formed his thoughts into words and sent two messengers to ask Jesus.

The Lord's reply is a splendid remedy for doubt: "Go back and report to John what you hear and see: The blind receive sight, the lame walk, those who have leprosy are cleansed, the deaf hear, the dead are raised, and the good news is proclaimed to the poor" (Matt. 11:4–5).

It's as if Jesus was saying, *John, remember what you saw. Look at what is happening now. God is still at work, even if you cannot see it.*

The new discoveries I had glimpsed were still out there. It's true in the spiritual realm too. I am forgiven. I am God's child. He is working in and through my life—and yours too. He still resides within us, remaking us in his image. Our failure to see change does not suggest God's failure to produce.

But I want to see. What did I want to see? If I wanted to experience my new sight, the solution was simple. Open my eyes, set foot out my door, and go see what there was to see.

> If you want to see what changes Jesus is bringing about in your life, how he interacts with you, and how he is involved in world events, be intentional.

What does a transformed life look like? What are the telltale signs of a forgiven soul? If you want to see what changes Jesus is bringing about in your life, how he interacts with you, and how he is involved in world events, be intentional. Initiate the search. Look in the right places. Like John, ask. *What are you doing, God? Show me.*

He would love to share. God wants you to notice what he has done and what he is doing. He loves it most when we ask, *What are you doing, Lord?*

And in the telling, both you and I will become Better Than Ever.

Lord, I don't want to take this life for granted.
Open my eyes. I want to see how you are
transforming me and changing the world.
Please show me.

SEEING WITH FRESH EYES

Write down what you've learned about God in the last week, how you've seen God at work in the lives of his people, and ways you've seen yourself live as God would have you live. If you've learned, changed, or observed in new ways, you've made progress in your salvation experience.

18

Hummingbird Wings

Since ancient times no one has heard, no ear has
perceived, no eye has seen any God besides you,
who acts on behalf of those who wait for him.
—ISAIAH 64:4

*M*y doctor told me to slow down. No new lens prescription until two months after surgery. Even then, my eyes would not fully stabilize for six months.

I wanted new and improved eyesight right away. *I have a life and I want to live it. I'm tired of figuring out what I can and can't do. I've had glimpses of what my new sight can do, and I want more. Have I said the word* now *yet?*

Does that describe the recovery seasons in your life? You want everything better now. You're tired of guessing, waiting, and sidestepping the land mines. A little consistency and predictability would let your brain take a power nap. Instead, responsibilities pile higher than the laundry, and you don't have the energy to keep up.

Others seem weary of your excuses. "I thought you were all healed. You were in church last Sunday. You're still in pain? Why are you so tired? Still wiped out by your divorce, your grief, or your [fill in the blank]? You should be . . ." The room echoes with unspoken expectations.

I'm a pastor's wife. I'm supposed to take care of everyone. *They must be tired of taking care of me*, I thought. So I ignored my healing body's warning bells and pushed through a wall of fatigue, determined I wouldn't let blurry eyes and a recovering body stop me.

It was too much too soon. I wasn't ready to do everything I thought I was supposed to do. And I grossly underestimated those who cared about me most.

After my saturation point overflowed into a tearful meltdown at a church function, Fergy took charge. "Clear your calendar on Thursday; we're taking you to a surprise destination."

That's what girlfriends do best. They see you at your worst and don't remind you of what you already know—that healing takes time. Instead, they help you through the process with grace and good humor.

Fergy, Carol, and Jule chose an isolated town that, unknown to them, I had wanted to visit for years. Bernadotte Café has a renowned charm—if you can find the place. Every window hosts a hummingbird feeder, and the owners must do something right because flocks of hummingbirds fight at every feeder and an equal number of customers vie for seats next to the windows.

I was grumpy. *I don't have my new glasses so I won't be able to see the birds. No, I don't want to sit next to the window, and don't point out the hummingbirds. I can't—*

Wait a minute.

"I can see its wings." My voice sounded flat, like a comment about the weather.

Jule's fork poised midair. "You can?"

My voice gained momentum. "I can." My mouth muscles tugged upward. "I've never seen a hummingbird before. But I can see its wings."

"Wow." The word ricocheted around the table faster than a hummingbird's dance, punctuated with the laughter of wonder and joy.

My food forgotten, I stared in fascination at a thumb-sized bird whose heart rate exceeded the miles per hour of a commercial jet.

It was another deposit on the promised gift of sight. A gift given slowly, in incremental portions so I could savor it one moment at a time, this time with cherished friends.

Like the hummingbird, a sparrow is fragile and vulnerable to the elements, demanding daily sustenance and shelter. Yet Jesus assured his followers that God cares about each sparrow that falls to the ground (Matt. 10:29). Didn't God care for my needs in my waiting time as well? This treasured small gift of hummingbird wings, needed for that moment, was my personal reminder of how much God knew and cared about what was happening to me. Better yet, he gave me friends who planned a surprise outing and who understood and rejoiced when he let me glimpse something I should not have been able to see.

Whatever you are dealing with in your own life, let me assure you: God cares about the moments you must spend in the healing process. He knows you need to gain strength before he can give you the unabridged version of your deepest desire. While you wait, he sends his comfort via his Spirit and in the form of good gifts as a deposit for the renewal he has in store for you. And he sends brothers and sisters in whom the Spirit also dwells to bear the burden with you and make the moments pass in peace.

Don't do your waiting moments alone.

Don't do your waiting moments alone. Tell God how you feel. He knows already anyway. Share your waiting season with select friends who are willing to hide you in back-road cafés so you can be grumpy among strangers and cry openly when God shows his love and awareness in small gifts like hummingbird wings.

Then you can pass the gift forward. Friends in the aftermath of grief or in the waiting hours of recovery need the same strength that sustained you. A visit, a word, moments of silent sitting may seem small to others. But you know that small gifts contain big value. When you simply wait, you are present for the time another of God's good gifts arrives. The blessing doubles because now your friend has someone to share the moment, someone who will rejoice with them at how God has given another sign of his loving care.

For good friends stand with each other in the waiting seasons.

Lord, open my eyes to see the good gifts you have for me during my hard moments, and the precious friends who enjoy those gifts with me.

SEEING WITH FRESH EYES

Who needs you to wait with them today? Take some flowers, a pot of soup, or a plate of cookies to a friend who is in a season of struggle. If possible, whisk them away to a different locale for a break from their ordeal. Give them the most precious gift of your time and companionship.

PART 3

SEEING WHAT GOD
WANTS ME TO SEE

19

Stars

*Lift up your eyes and look to the heavens: Who
created all these? He who brings out the starry
host one by one and calls forth each of them by
name. Because of his great power and mighty
strength, not one of them is missing.*
—ISAIAH 40:26

W hen I was a child, science and the Bible joined forces against my limited sight. Science recorded billions of stars in the night sky. God told the Old Testament patriarch Abraham that his descendants would rival the number of stars he could see. My dim eyesight doubted both. To me, the sky looked like nothing more than a canopy of dark with five pinpricks of light peering at me like beady bug eyes that laughed at my confusion. *Five wasn't very many people*, I dared to think whenever I heard the story of Abraham.

Now that I could see Better Than Ever, would more stars be visible? I rushed outside several nights in a row as the western sky faded to stare into the heavens, but weather, town lights, and a waxing gibbous moon kept me from stargazing. I would have to escape to the country after the full moon to verify the existence of stars.

I stood in the backyard of Bev's country home, waiting for my eyes to adjust to the dark. I lifted my face to the night sky and used my forefinger to count stars, losing my place in the counting. They spread across the sky like clouds of diamond dust displayed on dark velvet, congregating in groups to form intricate patterns. Clusters of white-shrouded crystals stretched from northwest to southeast in a wide banner I'd read about in books: the Milky Way.

It *was* true, oh so true. The night sky was far more beautiful, spacious, loaded, and brilliant than anything I could have ever imagined. I stood in the middle of that darkened yard and laughed with delight. I twirled around with my head thrown back till I was dizzy, trying to grasp in a few minutes what I had missed for so many years. I looked up and up and up, ordering my neck to stop complaining. "Wow," I could only utter. "Wow."

The heavens did declare the glory of God (Ps. 19:1). I danced in worship with a God who had the power, authority, and knowledge to create an expansive universe in all its scientific technicalities and artistic nuances.

I wonder if Abraham experienced the same conundrum of truth and perception I faced before Better Than Ever. God spoke with certainty; Sarah's empty arms told otherwise. Descendants as numerous as the stars? Really, God? Abraham saw only two sons on his star map—Isaac and Ishmael, and Ishmael didn't count, God said. Abraham's children by Keturah, the wife he married after Sarah died, didn't count either. Abraham died before Isaac's wife, Rebekah, gave birth to Jacob and Esau. He went to his grave seeing only a one-star glimpse of the promise fulfilled. One son. At least I had five stars. Yet, two generations later, Jacob's family numbered seventy; four hundred years after that, the record says the Israelites were as numerous as the stars (Deut. 1:10).

Even after Better Than Ever surgery, my vision is five times worse than a normally sighted person, and I still can't see as much of the night sky grandeur as most people do. Telescopes prove the universe extends far beyond what a normally sighted person can see. Yet the most powerful telescope reveals only a fraction of the breadth of the universe. All of us, not just those with limited sight, must accept on faith that the cosmos is more intricate, complex, and far-reaching than anything we can see or imagine.

Belief, or lack of belief, does not change truth.

Truth shines even if we don't see it or understand it. To refuse to believe in something merely because you don't see it would cause the skies to laugh, for even if you cannot see the stars, they are still there. Belief, or lack of belief, does not change truth. You don't need to see or understand to take God at his word—his creation is real, and he does keep his promises.

Why did God create more stars than we could possibly see? Perhaps he grants enough glimpses of reality to lure us to discover more. The trail of stars beckons us to pursue the Creator of the created. Yet, at some point, all of us will push against our human limitations. When we realize that more creation exists beyond our reach, we also discover there is far more to the understanding of God than we can ever begin to fathom. Some things, unseen, must be accepted on faith. Like Abraham, we accept the promise, trusting that God will be faithful to do all he said he would do.

What promises of God are at war with your perceptions? God says he is a God of justice who will destroy evildoers, but corruption, violence, and a cruel disregard for life seem to have become the rule rather than the exception. God promises to protect you and provide for you, but you or a loved one lie in a hospital bed, or you sit in front of a computer screen that shows records of an overdrawn bank account. God promises to always be with you, but you feel so alone.

Trust him. God's truth will win. God is at work, even if you cannot see or comprehend what he is doing. He exists and he is powerful, even if you can't make sense of your circumstances. The lack is on our end, not on his.

If you find yourself still questioning God's existence, despairing over his seeming lack of involvement, or confused about his plans and purposes, look at the sky and count the stars if you can. He made all of that and more, so much more beyond what you and I can see. The stars declare to us his glory and unlimited power. They give evidence of his existence and endless creativity. After our awe-filled season of star-gazing, we can go to bed with peace in our souls because God is in control and he is working in ways we cannot see. If he made the heavens so lavish and expansive, he will take care of us. And as he fulfilled his promise to Abraham, he will also keep the promises he has made to us.

Even if we cannot see him at work at the moment.

Lord, I declare that your creation is real and your Word is true, even if I cannot see or understand all that is. You will keep your promises. I trust your faithfulness to do what you have said you will do.

SEEING WITH FRESH EYES

Spend time outside on a clear night or visit a planetarium. What does the starry universe communicate to you about God's character and existence?

20

Sunrise

From the rising of the sun to the place where it
sets, the name of the LORD is to be praised.
—PSALM 113:3

*W*hat does it take to make a sunrise?

Seeing the Milky Way intensified my craving to take a fresh look at the world. What else had I missed? Nature beckoned me outside with the morning's first light.

I discovered that a sunrise is never static and God didn't create a world of still-life models. Like a wiggling five-year-old, sunrises won't hold still for the picture. Ever changing, they shift from deep purple to glowing gold and brilliant pinks until the sun appears on the horizon in a shout of glory.

Artists take months to create the thousands of frames needed for an animated motion picture, but God creates an in-motion sunrise with but one spoken word. Then he does it all over again the next day, splashing the sky with a new array of cloud and color. One day, gold hugs the line between heaven and earth. The next day, four-directional paint covers the eastern horizon.

The sun is always rising somewhere. God's rendition of a sunrise is so mammoth that every point on earth has its customized display. Bev, who lives less than two miles from me, sees a different sunrise than I do, and Cyndy, twelve miles farther, sees yet another.

Only God could mastermind the sunrise.

Think about the necessary components of a sunrise—light, color, vapor, gravity, dust and ash, temperature, and the angle of the earth's rotation. That silent sunrise contains massive amounts of energy and coordination. And then, God turned the earth into an amphitheater, for no stage is complete without an audience hall. Finally, he created the audience, people made in his image. He specifically designed our human eye and its connection to the brain to give us the ability to process, explore, and enjoy the unbounded treasures of the universe—stars, sunrises, sunsets, and so much more.

If God were on an MGM budget, he would have stuck with a more functional model. Sunrises don't have to look different every day. God could have made one design so everyone saw the same thing. He could have limited the cash flow on color, restricting it to only a few oranges and yellows.

What would be the fun of that? When you own it all, why spare expense?

He is not a practical God. His plan includes far more than shoving aside darkness to make room for light. He's going to rip back the curtain of night and explode the new day in all kinds of multicolored light. The brilliance of day won't sneak in like an unwelcome intruder. With a flourish of his almighty paintbrush, God says to us each morning, "Here's a new day. Ta-da!"

God did this for us. We are the capstone of his creation. Every day, art meets science, and God broadcasts his creativity, ingenuity, and authority across the eastern sky—for our viewing pleasure. The sunrise is a picture with a purpose, a perpetual testimony of God's unfailing love for us.

God wants us to use the sunrise as a memory prompt for something far more lavish. When Zechariah, the father of John the Baptist, spoke these words of prophecy, he linked the rising sun with the coming of the Messiah:

> And you, my child, will be called a prophet of the Most High;
> for you will go on before the Lord to prepare the way for him,
> to give his people the knowledge of salvation through the for-
> giveness of their sins, because of the tender mercy of our God,
> *by which the rising sun will come to us from heaven to shine on*
> *those living in darkness and in the shadow of death, to guide our*
> *feet into the path of peace.* (Luke 1:76–79, emphasis mine)

If God has been so extravagant with a sunrise, what about the gift of his Son?

Jesus comes to us in lavish layers of grace, peace, forgiveness, and love.

Jesus comes to us in lavish layers of grace, peace, forgiveness, and love. God spared no expense on our behalf. His unfailing love is as secure as the rising of the sun, which is sure to appear tomorrow morning, and the next, and the next. It will come in different colors and variants of light, for his mercies are new every morning (Lam. 3:22–23), new in a way that meets the ever-changing challenges of each day.

Go. Chase the sunrise. Revel in God's "Ta-da!" moment. And as you praise him for the beauty of the sunrise, praise him also for the lavish gift of his grace expressed through his Son, Jesus Christ.

Lord, your gift of grace is as spectacular as the
sunrise. Nothing can equal your glory. You did this
all for us. Thank you.

SEEING WITH FRESH EYES

God's mercies are new every morning, just like the sunrise. Today is a new day. Let go of yesterday's hurts and offenses and accept God's offer to start over again.

21

Flowers

As water reflects the face, so one's life
reflects the heart.
—PROVERBS 27:19

I donned my athletic shoes and opened my front door. One question filled my mind: What would I see on my morning walk that I couldn't see before? I lifted my head and dared to look beyond my six-foot bubble that for so long had restricted my sight to one section of sidewalk.

That day, I saw flowers. Not flower-lined driveway corners within touching range. I saw flowerpots set on porches, filled with brilliant blooms. Fuchsia-soaked pansies, curving rounded petals over the top of a terra-cotta pot.

I looked farther and saw more. Tall evergreens resembling the stance of tin soldiers from *The Nutcracker* ballet. Children's slides and picnic tables. Cobblestone paths leading from sidewalk to house. A plethora of detail filling every front and side yard, crafted to express the individual tastes of my neighbors. *People can see the stuff of a yard from the street? Oh dear, and I haven't planted my petunias yet.*

For years, my feet were my vehicle. Walks had a dual purpose of destination and exercise, but were seldom for pleasure because I couldn't see to enjoy. Intent on where to place my feet, I looked for nothing more than the next crack in the sidewalk. Passing car occupants assumed I was either rude for not acknowledging their hand wave, or pondering deep and mighty thoughts. Ah, if they only knew. My mind was debating more important matters, like whether that brown thing was a mud pile or a dead varmint.

Now I could see three sidewalk chinks ahead, giving me time to contemplate the world on either side. Curiosity reigned. What had I missed?

Trimmed hedges shaped into smooth curves. Swept walkways and low-level lighting. Flowers. More beautiful flowers.

I can see, I can see. My neighborhood is beautiful.

I'd assumed homeowners placed flowerpots on porches only for their own enjoyment. My opened eyes told the truth. Others saw my yard as I could see theirs. My garden flowers were as much for others as for myself. How I cultivated my flower beds and trimmed my yard was satisfying to both me and the steady stream of street travelers.

Scary thought. But perhaps that was a matter of perspective—a choice. I could choose to clean my yard out of fear of neighborly criticism, or I could create a pleasant place, enticing other pilgrims into the wonder of God's creation. I could be as intentional in sharing beauty with my neighbors as I was in finding it.

> As Christ followers, our task is twofold: look for God, and make it possible for others to find him too.

As Christ followers, our task is twofold: look for God, and make it possible for others to find him too. If we partner with him, God will use us to showcase his beauty.

Landscaping and home beautification projects don't have to be for our pleasure only. From flowerpots sitting on porches to flagstones placed in symmetrical patterns, our arrangement of nature calls out to those passing by who seek something to ponder and appreciate. It proclaims peace and extends an invitation to wonder and worship the Creator God. It fashions an environment of serenity so those who venture off the sidewalk can feel God's touch.

Creating your pleasant place doesn't have to be limited to yard art. That's a good thing, because I'm not a very good gardener. We can form beauty in our home, our kitchen, or our welcoming spirit. Even plunking a hyacinth in a self-watering pot and letting God give the increase allows a bit of creation to declare God's glory to the passerby.

So we plant flowers in pots, add butterfly bushes to roadsides, fill kitchens with the scent of sweet cinnamon and baking bread, line shelves with good books, put cups of steaming coffee in cold hands, and speak kind words to broken hearts. We become conduits of God's grace so others have the chance to see Christ at work within us, the hope of heaven's glory to come (Col. 1:27). We add wonders of God's creation and symbols of joy to our life's landscape so others will find the God they are chasing. And in the sharing, we find God anew, for we have partnered with him to brag on his existence.

I wonder if it's too late to plant my petunias.

Lord God, show me yourself today so I can see you anew. Then help me reflect what I see so others can see you too.

SEEING WITH FRESH EYES

Take stock of what you like to do best. How can you use your passions to declare God's glory, existence, and peace to those who connect with you?

22
Clouds

For now we see only a reflection as in a mirror;
then we shall see face to face. Now I know in
part; then I shall know fully, even as I am fully
known.
—1 CORINTHIANS 13:12

*A*ssumptions are dangerous.

The perceptions we gain in childhood can lull us into taking our world as we see it for granted. As adults, we fall into the trap of failing to think twice about a matter if we've convinced ourselves that we have seen all there is to see.

That's the way I was with clouds.

And I was so wrong.

When I was a child, clouds looked like nothing more than white smudges on a blue canvas. Detail and depth were nonexistent. I outranked Charlie Brown from the comic strip *Peanuts*. While his friend Linus saw moments from history etched in the clouds, Charlie Brown saw simple things like duckies and horsies.

I saw blobs.

The sky looked flat too. Maybe the earth was flat. I shrugged and went on with life, not giving much thought to clouds or pondering whether Charlie Brown or flat-earthers were right.

I didn't know what I was missing until I could see more.

Since Better Than Ever, I've discovered hundreds of stars, vivid sunrises, and detailed dirt clods. What else could be different about my world? One look upward and I found clouds. Full and substantive masses, yet lightweight enough for wind to sweep them into new formations, ever changed and ever changing. Heavy-bottom cumulous clouds, pregnant with moisture, highlighted by feathered cirrus strands thousands of feet above. The detail stirred my curiosity; the artistry unlocked my imagination. There really were duckies. And whales and train engines and the Leaning Tower of Pisa.

I joined the ranks of weather watchers and inventive children, eager to find what form the clouds would take each day, craving to uncover truths the sky held about my Creator God. And I was so grateful. Grateful for clouds and rain and eyesight and . . . What a wonderful world.

All of us enter adulthood with preconceived notions and incomplete knowledge. We laugh at flat-earthers, yet each of us has had seasons of two-dimensional thinking. Truth gets a passing nod as we forget or refuse to examine the deeper details about God, the world he has established, history within the span of eternity, or the grace Christ so freely offers.

Do you find yourself accepting any of these ideas?

Traditional marriage doesn't work.

Looks are everything.

The church is a country club of legalistic dos and don'ts.

I am unlovable: I exist only to be controlled or used.

We coast through life, taking for granted what we've been told or what we think we've seen without applying the effort to believe otherwise. But when we do stop to examine creation, life, and God's rational order of things, delightful treasures beckon us to look at life in new ways. We pause in wonder and gratitude, worshipping a God who is like no other.

Like sunlight pouring through a hole in the clouds, creating sun-beams on the earth beneath, God longs to shine his reality on your worldview, inviting you to look up, see, and experience the greater view of what he is like and how he intends life to be.

Those flat-earth perceptions I listed above? God's truth says this:

Marriage is an awesome thing if done God's way.

The greatest value is found in a person's character.

The church is a place of grace, love, and acceptance, an earthly reflection of Christ.

Jesus loves you lavishly, enough to forfeit his life for you.

What childhood assumptions do you still hold about the world, relationships, or the place of the church in God's scheme of things? What were you told when you were a child about who you are or who God is? What blurry, misshapen image of yourself do you still cling to that is not really accurate? For example, did someone write a hurtful message in your eighth-grade yearbook that you still believe is a true assessment of your character?

It takes courage and time to step aside from the ordinary routine and ask, "What's out there? What does God want me to see?"

Look into the sky and see those three-dimensional clouds. Life has far more nuance and depth than a blob of white. The world is more. You are more; God is more. Who you were decades ago, what you were taught to believe may not be necessarily so. And if it isn't true, you can—you need to—let it go.

How? Look deep into God's Word, the Bible. His truth is unchanging. It is reliable because it is unchanging. When you find truth that doesn't agree with what you've come to accept and believe, ask God to give you the motivation to change your thinking and then start living according to the worldview he's expressed in his Word.

Let me warn you. It takes courage and time to step aside from the ordinary routine and ask, "What's out there? What does God want me to see, and how does he want me to see it?" But it's worth it. God promises he will instruct you and teach you in the way you should go (Ps. 32:8). Paul encouraged his readers to allow God to transform their minds so they could know God's perfect will (Rom. 12:2). If God can alter my eyesight to see three-dimensional clouds instead of white smudges with purple bellies, he can transform your thinking to see him as he really is and his world as he intended it to be.

The freedom you will find is absolutely wonderful. You'll lie on your back, soak up the sunshine of his love for you, and imagine all sorts of patterns in the clouds of what his plans for you might look like.

After all, God is so much more than we can see or imagine.

Lord, I'm ready to see you, myself, and my world as you see. Teach me what reality looks like. Lure me toward your creation so I can pause and ponder what it tells me about who you are.

SEEING WITH FRESH EYES

On a slip of paper, write a misconception you have about God or yourself. Tear the paper in pieces and throw it away. Ask God to remind you of the truth when you slip back into old patterns of thinking.

23

Autumn Leaves

You will go out in joy and be led forth in peace;
the mountains and hills will burst into song before
you, and all the trees of the field will clap
their hands.
—ISAIAH 55:12

As children, we didn't mind the leaves of fall. Oblivious to our parents' warnings about what might lurk in those piles—dog excrement, bugs, other creepy critters, or germs in general—we buried each other, made forts, and tossed handfuls in the air.

Adulthood requires that we sober our playful spirits and turn our attention to the responsibility of leaf removal. We reluctantly get out the rakes and lawn mowers to clean up the mess, grumbling about autumn's extra work. The lawn looks lovely until the neighbor's neglected yard waste blows over the fence. Falling leaves and bare limbs are almost as depressing as the day the Christmas tree comes down.

Baxter, our Welsh corgi, didn't think so.

One windy, cold, and cloudy day, I took Baxter out for his noontime outing. My Pembroke Welsh corgi's nickname was ADD—Attention Deficit Doggie. The *deficit* part was in full throttle that day as he abandoned one airborne leaf for another in quick succession. His lean body suspended in space like a hindquarter of beef in a freezer locker as he tried to catch a leaf midair. Then he scampered after a foraging squirrel and ran circles around a new swirl of falling debris, grinning bigger than a child with a wad of Silly Putty. He was having a blast.

With an impatient sigh, I kept my feet away from the leash that had morphed into a swinging jump rope. Secretly, I wished I could be like my dog. No other care in the world than to chase after leaves and invite the squirrels to play. How lovely to view leaves as playthings, not as one more chore. But I was an adult and I had a waiting to-do list.

Come on, Baxter, let's head for the house. I'm cold.

But, Mommy, see the leaves? They twirl and swirl. I can twirl and swirl too—watch me. You'd be warmer if you danced with me.

Yes, Baxter, I see the leaves.

I paused, soon oblivious to the leash wrapping around my feet. *I do see the leaves.*

That first October after the Better Than Ever surgery had already let me witness autumn in all its wonder like I'd never seen it before. Trees were no longer solid blobs of color. From fifty feet away, I could see the variegated patterns of gold, orange, yellow, and still green, displaying various levels of decay. Red Heart couldn't have produced a lovelier skein of multicolored yarn.

But that moment with Baxter presented something new. I could see single leaves falling from tree to ground. If you had asked me before my eye surgery, I would have said watching leaves fall was as entertaining as waiting for the microwave to beep. I never thought observing leaves dance in a final descent could be downright fun until I watched Baxter. Now I stood trancelike, mesmerized by nature's choreography and wishing I was as uninhibited as my dog is in joining the autumn dance.

Why not dance among the leaves? Why not take time to play and praise and ponder this part of creation?

While Baxter stretched for another mouthful, I mulled over God's design for this season of the year. Why did the Lord make autumn linger over a six-week stretch, letting leaves take their sweet time to change color and drop to the ground? He could have constructed the season so all leaves would fall on one day. He could have decreed, say, October 21 as the official Leaf Drop Day. Plunk. Whoosh. Down. Okay, everyone, October 22 is National Pick Up the Leaves Day. Stay home and rake leaves. Guaranteed perfect leaf-raking weather too. Let's get those leaf blowers out and get 'er done so we can move on to the next event on the calendar. Don't forget the apple cider.

How boring.

Our God is wildly creative, imaginative, and surprising. He sends the wind so leaves can dance, and dogs and children can play and chase. So adults like me can pause in wonder, revel in the gift of color, and live vicariously through the capers of pets and kids.

Or maybe not so vicariously. Perhaps God is calling us, his children, to step from the sidelines, drop our reserve, and join the celebration.

Our God is not an all-work-and-no-play God. His creation declares how lavish his love is for us. And he takes delight in watching his children utter unrestrained praise. That kind of unbridled honor speaks of a heart unequivocally relinquished to him. Praise that streams forth from more than duty. It disregards the muck and mire of ritual and tradition. It jives through the privacy of a living room or down the center aisle of a public worship service in free-form dance. It looks askance at others' opinions or reactions to our style of praise. Instead, there's a freedom to worship with only the thought of expressing unadulterated joy for who God is and what he has done.

God is worth every expression of praise you can give him, and he loves it when you express it with total abandon.

That's how David worshipped when the ark of the covenant came home to Jerusalem. David stripped off the weightier clothes of his royal position that constrained his movements, became like the common man or maid, and danced before the Lord "with all his might" (2 Sam. 6:14). It didn't matter that his wife Michal wasn't impressed. David's joy at God's goodness knew no bounds, and David expressed his praise with every muscle in his body.

What constrains you from giving God uninhibited praise? Perhaps you don't know where to start. Let the leaves teach you. Or the sunrise, a perfect cloudless day, or gently falling snow. Disregard what others might think. Focus totally on God as your audience of one, and be yourself. You might dance. Or you might whisper an adoring, *I love you, Lord*. Whatever you do, do more than you've done. Because God is worth every expression of praise you can give him, and he loves it when you express it with total abandon.

With a furtive glance toward my neighbor's yard, I did a pirouette in front of an oak tree, caught a falling leaf, and put it in my pocket so the glory would never fade away. I lifted my arms toward heaven, leash in hand, and praised the Maker of wind, leaves, hyperactive puppy dogs, and eyes to see. Then I called a confused Baxter into the house.

King David would probably say it was a good start.

Lord, fill me with such joy over your creation and your work in the world that I want to burst into song and dance, for you are worthy of passionate, impulsive praise that knows no limits.

SEEING WITH FRESH EYES

What inspires you to spontaneous praise? Find time today to seek out a setting that will inspire your praise of God the Creator.

24

Holly Berries

Show me your ways, LORD, teach me your paths.
—PSALM 25:4

Jack drove our rental car down a narrow road in Atlanta's famed Westview Cemetery, fretting that we wouldn't make it in time for his mother's graveside service. I shared his angst. *How much farther? When will we get there?* My eyes focused on the dashboard, my mind on the destination.

Obsessing over the time crunch during a road trip is nothing new for me. I always think about the ETA when I'm in a car. When everything outside is a blurry blur, what is there to do? The cliché childhood question "Are we there yet?" is understandable for someone who can't see out the window. If you can't see, you don't know. If it's a long trip and you can't enjoy the process, you sink into ambivalence and tend to forget that a world exists outside. You think your own thoughts, converse with other people inside the car, sleep, or put in earbuds. The car becomes your life-sphere.

My mind was focused on one thing that dreary, brown December day in Westview Cemetery. One event. Nothing more. *Are we there yet?*

Then I saw holly berries.

Isn't it so good that God created a plant that produces red berries at the same time trees become bare and fall edges toward winter? A bright splash of color against the season's gray, red in stark relief against the brown of matted grass, flecked with white snow. The perfect size for a hungry bird's beak. Free nature-ware for holiday decorations.

I can see holly berries.

Outside-car-window vision kicked in. What else could I see? Trees with scrappy leaves, resistant to the tug of the wind. Tombstones and flattened flower arrangements. Hills and winding roads. More holly berries. What perfect timing to be in this place just as the berries turned from green to red. My world expanded beyond my thoughts about the graveside service, and I caught creation's hint of heaven. *Thank you, God.* What would I have missed if I had refused to look out the window?

Other journeys have taken place since that December day, and I still find myself retreating into my turtle shell, thinking only about what waits at the journey's end. *Are we there yet? Conquer the miles. Let's get this transition over with so we can get on to what's next.* And I forget to look out my window.

But holly berries whisper a liberating message: the journey is as important as the destination, and there is more to life than what is ahead. God plants his creation along our path so we can catch glimpses of his ever-increasing glory, a sneak preview of the wonder of Eden restored.

God invites you and me to walk with him and see the great and mighty things we would miss if we weren't looking.

"Your will be done, on earth as it is in heaven" (Matt. 6:10). If I'm not looking for God's will on this earth, I won't notice the secrets it shares about the final destination of heaven. Using the bright red of berries or other creation splendor as his visual megaphone, God invites you and me to walk with him and see the great and mighty things we would miss if we weren't looking.

The apostle Paul expressed this attitude to the church in Philippi when he reflected upon where he was compared to where he wanted to be. He wanted Jesus to be exalted through his life, whether in daily living or through his death: "To live is Christ and to die is gain" (Phil. 1:21). The destination of heaven was worth his pursuit, but until then, he could find delight in the beautiful fruit his work with the churches produced, even though at the time he was in a prison cell.

You too can make your life journey more memorable. Look for mementos of roadside wonder that remind you of God's purposes for you right here, right now. Appreciate what you have and hold in this moment rather than fixating on what you might not have tomorrow. Make the most of every day by initiating conversations with new friends and beloved family en route to your next daily destination. Resist the temptation to lock your vision in focal-point format and, instead, notice what lies at the edges of your eyesight. Think less about your upcoming arrival and more about what is happening in the present. Look for God at work in the whirling moments that slip into the past all too quickly.

God has a world of great and mighty things he put in place just for you. You might find holly berries. And a lot more.

Lord, forgive me when I've succumbed to tunnel vision, wasting precious time in anxious thoughts over the next event rather than making use of the moment you've given me. Thank you for how the simple parts of your creation remind me of the beauty and importance of this day.

SEEING WITH FRESH EYES

As you head toward your next daily destination, look for three things on the journey that remind you of God's presence and love for you.

25

Ocean Waves

Mightier than the thunder of the great waters,
mightier than the breakers of the sea—the LORD on
high is mighty.
—PSALM 93:4

I stood at an ocean's edge for the first time since Better Than Ever.
I could see rolling waves, pounding surf, the glisten of sun on the
water's surface, and froth spilling over itself to claw at the beach, all
in 3D definition. I inched my toes forward, daring the surf to wash
over them, then squealed like a five-year-old when salt water splashed
my face too. Relentless waves tumbled and turned, pushing water in a
never-ending pattern of new places, taunting those braver than me to
venture into its undertow.

What intense power. It seemed like nothing could stop the ocean
from coming ashore.

While I was delighted that I could see details of the ocean, those
relentless waves painted a picture of my season of life. Wave after wave
had rolled over our family: job turmoil, unstable friendships, health
issues, and family loss. The final wrench to our hearts came when we
had to say goodbye to our dog, Baxter, for the last time. Despondent,

we left for a vacation to visit our oldest daughter, Katherine, who now lived near the ocean, but storm-delayed flights caused us to reach her home twenty-four hours after our original arrival time.

Would the storms ever stop?

As a white-capped wave hurled toward my feet, I cried out to the Lord: *I can't do this anymore. I can't take any more.*

At the last moment, the wave stopped short of my toes and receded, sucked back into the ocean. Mesmerized, I watched wave after wave. Some came farther than others, but always, at some point, they retreated. Every single one came only so far. Some unseen force restrained them. It was the way God made the ocean to be.

Oh yes, there are hurricanes that drive sea surges farther inland. The very next week after we left, that particular beach was forever reformed by Hurricane Florence. The seas "lifted up their voice" in that storm (Ps. 93:3). And yet, there was still a certain point where they went no farther. The overflow of the Cape Fear River pushed toward Katherine's house. At one point, halfway up the hill, it stopped and turned back.

After the granddaddy of all floods, God told Noah, "Never again will there be a flood to destroy the earth" (Gen. 9:11). God never pledged the absence of storms. He did not say there would never be loss of life or property. He said that floodwaters would never totally destroy the earth as it had in Noah's day. Someday, the Lord will bring his final judgment upon the earth in the form of annihilation. But total destruction won't happen until he brings his children safely home. Until that time, like the sign of the ocean wave, there will always be a measure of restraint. As bad as life might get, there will always be a point for now when God says, "No more."

The sea belongs to God, for he is the one who made it (Ps. 95:5). He created the barrier of beach that restricts the sea: "The waves may roll, but they cannot prevail; they may roar, but they cannot cross it" (Jer. 5:22). And God spelled out his limits on the sea to Job in no uncertain terms: "Who shut up the sea behind doors when it burst forth from the womb, when I made the clouds its garment and wrapped it in thick darkness, when I fixed limits for it and set its doors and bars in place, when I said, 'This far you may come and no farther; here is where your proud waves halt'?" (Job 38:8–11).

You and I may put a magnifying glass over the troubles of our lives, wondering why God allows us to suffer so much hardship. Fearful that we aren't strong enough to bear the brunt of the storm. Questioning if God didn't get the memo that he wouldn't give us any more than we could handle. I've caught myself saying, "God must think I'm stronger than I think I am, because this is more than I think I can take."

Truth says God will give us no more than he can handle.

The same God who made the sea created our lives. The God powerful enough to create is also powerful enough to sustain. Because we are his prime creation, God cares exponentially more about us than about a beachfront. The same unseen hand that pushes the waves into their proper place also controls our life circumstances, all while working together those difficulties for a bigger purpose. "We are hard pressed on every side, but not crushed," Paul wrote in 2 Corinthians 4:8, "perplexed, but not in despair."

If you have suffered multiple losses and wondered if God has deserted you, it's okay to question and grieve. But God also promises that "rejoicing comes in the morning" (Ps. 30:5). There is an end to overwhelming grief and the unintended consequences of injustice. Your current trouble may ebb away within a few months. Or the end will come when you transition from earth to eternity. Ultimately, all evil will end when Christ comes again.

Are you still not convinced? I know. It's hard to believe there is anyone in control when the waves keep washing over your life, getting bigger and stronger. But God is in control and you have not lost everything. You would not be reading these pages if all were lost. Have you seen God provide for your needs? Has he given you strength, wisdom, and guidance beyond what you know is normal for you? What do you still have? Family, friends, a roof over your head, a gift of groceries? All those things show that God's hand has restrained the wave that would love to suck you—and everything and everyone with you—down into the depths.

God is still with you, giving you everything you need so you can ride the waves rather than succumb to their undertow. And one day, in the near or distant future, he will say, "No more."

Until God's chosen end point, he lends his unlimited strength to you so you can stand firm against what seeks to destroy your faith and confidence in God. While it may not seem like it in the moment, God plants sweet reminders that he is indeed in control of whatever happens and that he has established the mark at which trouble will go no further.

> Our Lord will not give you any more than he and you can manage together.

He is stronger than the strongest of storms and mightier than anything you will face. He is more powerful than any sickness or trial. He has more resources than any corporate slush fund and more compassion than any family member who, in their own weak moment, can still let you down. Our Lord will not give you any more than he and you can manage together. Your struggle may sabotage your health, destroy your finances, or level your home. But if you cling to Jesus, whatever trial you face cannot destroy your relationship with him.

What waves do you fear? What force would love to destroy your body, soul, and spirit? Keep moving forward with your day and throw your worries on the God who has control. Let the roar of the sea be in God's capable hands. For he stands at the corners of the earth, drawing back the undertow that could pull you under. He holds sway over anything that threatens to engulf you.

He has given you his word.

Lord, a tsunami of trouble seems headed my way.
Fear tempts me to succumb to its power. You alone
can restrain its ability to destroy my spirit. I trust

that, when this is over, your strong hand will still
hold mine, keeping me upright. Help me.

SEEING WITH FRESH EYES

Name a current overwhelming situation or one you fear may happen. Envision it as an ocean wave racing toward you. Dig your heels into the ground, clench your teeth, and remind yourself that you and God can face it together and that he has the resources to see you through.

26

Geese

The earth is the LORD's, and everything in it,
the world, and all who live in it.
—PSALM 24:1

As I opened my mailbox one morning, the honking of geese filled the western horizon. Geese in February? My hand perched over my eyes as I strained to see in the direction of the sound. Since I'd never seen more than black flecks that could have been flies or floaters, I'd put seeing geese in flight on my Better Than Ever bucket list. Now was my chance.

The sound grew louder. The geese must be moving in my direction. Interest morphed into an excitement befitting a five-year-old, bouncing on her heels.

Daddy, Daddy, I want to see the geese. Pleeeeese?

Rest assured, I was a little more adult than that. But not by much. *Oh, God, I would like to see the geese. It would be so nice if they came closer.* Was it a prayer or a wish? Good thing we live on a quiet street. I may have spoken the words out loud.

And the Lord, in his extravagant love, said, *Sure.*

Within seconds, a dark cloud materialized and flew east about fifty feet directly over my head. Thousands of geese stretched for miles in lines straighter than I could ever draw. The whites of their bellies reflected the late morning sun and their dark wings outstretched as if in praise to their Creator.

I know because I saw it for myself.

I learned later the white underbellies and parallel lines, rather than the more common *V* formation, identified them as snow geese, who like to forage in barren farmlands before planting season. Do they usually fly that close to the ground? I never found out. The amazing coincidence was that they flew directly over my street. Not a mile to the north or even a block to the south, but right over my head.

Serendipity? Maybe not. In fact, I don't believe that one bit. It was as if God gave them a map of my town and ordered, "Follow this road."

Could God cause a line of geese to stream across the sky at one specific latitude just so one human could see geese for the first time? Sure. He can do that kind of thing. If God has the power to create an animal, he can overwrite its instincts. If Jesus could direct wind and waves with but one command, he has the authority to move an entire line of geese.

But *would* he do such a thing for one woman who couldn't even script her desire into a formalized prayer request? Who sounded more like an overeager child hopping from one foot to the other instead of a mature, devoted disciple?

God loves our enjoyment of his creation. He delights to give us good gifts.

God loves our enjoyment of his creation. He delights to give us good gifts. If he was willing to give the precious gift of his Son, Jesus Christ, wouldn't he want to also give us all good things (Rom. 8:32)?

What do you want to see? Does it sound too far-fetched, too small, maybe even a tad selfish? Would the natural laws of creation need to bend for it to happen? Would the normal ways of doing business or institutional procedures have to glitch for you to see God at work?

That's no problem for God. He who created nature and crafted people in his image has the infinite skill to literally move heaven and earth to make it happen. God does not specialize only in miracles of healing, like my eye surgery. He can do anything. He can do it because he is God. When we ask God to do something beyond the laws of nature or simply beyond the normal ebb and flow of everyday life, we become like that innocent, trusting five-year-old who believes Daddy can do anything. We confirm our belief in God's limitless power when we bother to ask. And we prove that we believe he is interested in the little stuff as much as we are. Because he is.

Sometimes all it takes is a wistful wish the size of a mustard seed, and God is on it.

My friend Tina wished her parents would reconcile. After their divorce, they had each remarried, but now both second partners had passed on. The hostility was enormous and far-reaching. If one parent planned to attend a family event, the other was sure not to come.

Tina kept praying. For years, she begged her mother to go to church, forgive, and let the past go. Finally, Tina's mom admitted she was ready to seek God because she wanted the joy she saw in her daughter's life. She wrote a note of apology to her ex-husband.

Then God fulfilled the unspoken wish. Fifty years after their divorce, acting like lovestruck teenagers, Tina's parents announced their engagement for remarriage. "I never dreamed they would get back together," Tina told me. "Just having them be civil with each other would have been a miracle. I think God was telling me I didn't pray big enough."

Can God move a line of geese? Yes. Can he restore a broken marriage? Beyond what we can possibly imagine. If God can alter nature, he can move within hearts and minds. It may be unseen to us. It may not happen for years or in our lifetime. But the first step is for us to agree that *God can*. And if it's in his best plan for us, he is delighted to do it for us.

Ask. Watch. When you see it happen, don't chalk it up to coincidence. Give credit where credit is due, for you just saw God alter the normal. He loves you enough to give you the impossible. He does the miraculous because he is God and he wants to be known for being a God like no other. Yes, he might say no. He might say wait. But those responses shouldn't hinder our asking. Because he just might say yes. And we will be utterly amazed.

For God, being God, can do those kinds of things.

Lord, I ask, not for my own enjoyment or
convenience. I want to witness the way you work.
When I see what you can do, it further convinces
me that you are God and you control the universe.

SEEING WITH FRESH EYES

What have you seen God do beyond the ordinary? Stop and thank him that he is able to do such things. Thank him for being God.

27

Snow

He says to the snow, "Fall on the earth," and to
the rain shower, "Be a mighty downpour." So that
everyone he has made may know his work, he
stops all people from their labor.
—JOB 37:6–7

It's snowing!"

I saw it snow. Not a white mass on the ground after the snowstorm had passed. My eyes caught the sight of the white stuff in the air. Large, fluffy clumps of snow. Groups of snowflakes banding together to stay warm or show team spirit, if snowflakes do such a thing. A fine mist of baby snowflakes scheming to group-bomb the earth, enveloping the ground in a conquering blanket of white.

Then there's the snowfall of abandonment, each snowflake dancing to the whim of a relentless wind. Some flakes nose-dive to the ground in a ruthless death spiral to accomplish their destiny. Others balk, defying the law of gravity, as they barter with the wind's updraft and choose to play along the way.

Don't close the book or skip to the next chapter. I understand. You may have a vastly different viewpoint about snow. Facebook friends were not impressed with my childlike delight and poetic prose either. Several depicted the snow as inconvenient, unpleasant, and downright dangerous. "Here's your snow," one friend captioned a picture of a fifty-car pileup in East Tennessee.

I'm sorry you see the snow as deadly, I wanted to write back.

I wish life responsibilities didn't have to pull us onto dangerous roads and expose us to sinus-numbing cold. It would be lovely if everyone could stay home and build snow forts, watch the children ambush each other with snowballs, and drink hot chocolate. Older folks could draw circles with their boot toes without worry of an ankle-shattering fall. Unfortunately, we have lives to live and we can't always let snow delay our day's plans.

The truth remains. Snow is beautiful, one of God's incredible creations. Snow was only one part of that pileup. Cars with worn tires, unplowed roads, and human error all factored into that heart-wrenching collision.

I can hear you thinking: *If the snow had not been there in the first place, it wouldn't have been so deadly.* Why would God create something with such harmful potential?

Anything good can be corrupted into bad. Mix God's untarnished creation with the destructive composite of sin that mars our earth, and nature becomes toxic. Even salt and water can be overused and abused. The same water that acts as a life-nourishing drink can move with hurricane force that, coupled with the intensity of wind, can destroy entire cities. Ask New Orleans. It can capsize boats and drown innocent children. But I still drink water. I need it to survive.

The Sonoran Desert in southwestern Arizona is one of the most verdant arid regions in the world. It is full of life and has a rugged beauty to it. Yet to the unprepared, it is stuffed with deadly peril: rattlesnakes, scorpions, tarantulas, and nasty spine-infested cacti.

Why, God? Why did you create these things that could harm people, your favorite part of creation?

God made a world that is bigger than us. Intrinsically, we appreciate the power of the storm, the energy of lightning, and the mass of a mountain. If those things did not hold power, they would no longer be what they are and they would not speak to us of God's unlimited power. All of nature would have a limp beauty, ever fragile and quickly conquered. Mankind would be lured into a God complex more than we already are.

The God of creation is the most powerful thing in the universe. He is still in charge, and he has the power and love to protect us and pull us through.

But the mass of a mountain, the force of the wind, and even too many snowflakes are a simple reminder that there are more powerful things in the world than me. They affirm that the God of creation is the most powerful thing in the universe. He is still in charge, and he has the power and love to protect us and pull us through.

Our response is a matter of perspective. We can choose to see the beauty and appreciate God's incredible creativity, or we can magnify the danger and question his sensibilities. Slippery roads, inconvenient delays, and backbreaking snow removal can be God's little wake-up call that we aren't as fully in control as we'd like to think we are.

Each of us has struggled at one time or another against a force of nature, a life situation, or the cemented boundaries of a bureaucracy that is bigger than ourselves, one that with but a single glimpse raises our stress level. We'd like to control that power source. We'd like to not feel out of control. Maybe your bugaboo is fire, windstorms, or brown recluse spiders. The best you and I can do as humans is to manage our interactions with nature's force to minimize its danger potential and to appreciate once again the kind of powerful God we worship and serve. God created fire, snow, water, and the energy of a lightning bolt. Each exists for us to enjoy while also respecting the power they hold.

Yes, God can make something both beautiful and powerful. It's more evidence of the kind of capable, loving, creative, and awesome God that he is.

God, forgive me for the times I have questioned the goodness of your creation and seen it as harmful or inconvenient. The next time I encounter nature's forces that are stronger than me, remind me that you are still greater and that you can protect me from any danger.

SEEING WITH FRESH EYES

The next time you become perturbed at nature's inconvenience, pause to ponder that God created it to be that way, and he also created power and energy. Remind yourself of the good that power can bring, and thank God for all that makes his creation stunning and complex.

28

Blood Moon

The heavens declare the glory of God;
the skies proclaim the work of his hands. Day after
day they pour forth speech; night after night they
reveal knowledge.
—PSALM 19:1–2

A bitter wind blew one January morning as my silent husband, still in his sleeping shirt and sweatpants, headed out the front door. I took notice because doing anything before his first cup of coffee is not normal. I didn't have a chance to ask, "What are you doing?"

Upon returning, Jack jerked a thumb toward the door. "There's a lunar eclipse out there."

My phone chimed. *If you're awake, there's a lunar eclipse going on right now*, my friend Cyndy wrote.

A lunar eclipse at predawn? It must have been something special for two people to mention it. I trekked outside and forgot it was cold.

A supermoon, painted copper and capped with a shiny white sliver, hung in the western sky. For thirty minutes, using a small monocular telescope, I watched the white crescent fade into burnished red. What a gift to see an eclipse that occurs at most twice a year—if you're in the right spot, under a cloudless sky, and awake without coffee. It was something I had never seen before. And this one was extra special.

God had to go to a lot of trouble to design the mechanics for a lunar eclipse.

As I braced against a cold wind and stared at the moon, two questions came to mind. First, why does a lunar eclipse, also known as a blood moon, happen so seldom? And, second, why did astronomers take so long to figure out the why and how of it?

God made the sun, moon, and earth to be the exact diameter and distance they need to be from each other so that when the earth passes between the other two, the earth's shadow fits neatly over the moon. During a total eclipse, the sun's rays refract around the earth and create the reddish glow we see. Then God put the moon on an elliptical course so lunar eclipses would be more random than regular.

What a curious choice. Why did God assign a random pattern to lunar eclipses? Perhaps because that irregularity catches our attention and gives us something to anticipate. The occasional but predictable schedule makes us mark our calendars, set our alarm clocks, and leave our houses at odd hours to snap pictures and try to wrap our brains around how such a wonderful thing could happen. It causes us to look.

Scientists took centuries to figure out the mechanics of a lunar eclipse. Babylonians in 745 BC first predicted when the next eclipse would occur but didn't know how or why it happened. In the early sixteenth century, Christopher Columbus intimidated Jamaican natives into supplying provisions for his crew by accurately predicting the next eclipse. Frightened by a phenomenon they didn't understand, the natives brought Columbus all he wanted.

Why would God allow humanity to misunderstand his creation for centuries? Even now, we cannot grasp the expanse of the universe. The Bible doesn't help much. The creation record in Genesis 1 gives only a sketchy blueprint of the solar system. Verse 16 says, "God made two great lights—the greater light to govern the day and the lesser light to govern the night. He also made the stars." That's all. No measurements, design models, or prototypes.

Even though it took scientists millennia to find a fraction of all that is in the universe, God left the mysteries of the heavens for us to discover. Why?

The more intensive the search, the more exhilarating the discovery. The expansive universe that we have uncovered merely shows how much we still don't know. We could spend lifetimes exploring the heavens and still fall short of knowing all there is to know.

That's the way God planned it to be. If God had designed a universe with discernible limits or if he himself could be known in his fullness, he would no longer be God. And we, in turn, would want to push him off the throne of his sovereignty.

Only God has the skill and wisdom to make a perfectly ordered cosmos. The precise order, detail, and predictability of things like eclipses, meteor showers, and comets challenge the random chance of evolutionary theory. The sky's aesthetic beauty mocks the limits of scientific reasoning. The universe shouts of a Creator behind the creation. A show too big to miss and too grand to ignore catches the attention of those who deny the existence of God and challenges them to reconsider.

I remember watching news footage of the August 21, 2017, total solar eclipse. One viewer after another could hardly describe their reactions to what they saw. They shook their heads and used one-word descriptions like "incredible" and "phenomenal." Unable to state belief in a divine Creator, they still found it spectacular.

God uses the expansive features of the sky as his calling card, introducing humanity to himself as the artist behind the creation.

The Bible says that those without access to the biblical record are offered the chance to understand God's existence through the witness of creation (Rom. 1:20). God uses the expansive features of the sky as his calling card, introducing humanity to himself as the artist behind the creation, the God who is more unlimited than the never-ending universe.

Check out the date of the next lunar or solar eclipse. Get up early or set your alarm clock for the middle of the night if you must. As you look, ask yourself, *What do planetary rotations tell me about God?* If you ponder long enough, I think you'll come to the same conclusion I did. There is no way a lunar or solar eclipse could happen by chance. Only a divine craftsman with infinite power, authority, and wisdom could put the universe together with such perfection and grandeur.

Chase an eclipse once and it will become habit-forming. The lure of a lunar eclipse will beckon you from your warm home into the cold morning air and cause you to consider the one, the only infinitely powerful and wise one, who could plan and execute such a perfect design. It will make you think about who God is in comparison to yourself.

That's what happens to me. As I watch these incredible heavenly events, suddenly God seems so big and I seem so small. I realize how much he is God and how much I am not. And as I stare at the burnished red of a blood moon, worship spills out of my mouth with but one word.

Wow.

Only God. Like no one else.

Lord, may I continue to discover truths about the
world you have made, so each time I can pause
and worship you as Creator God.

SEEING WITH FRESH EYES

Plan to observe a solar or lunar eclipse, a meteor shower, or a comet. What do these occurrences tell you about God?

PART 4

SEEING WHO GOD WANTS ME TO SEE

29

Faces

Look to the LORD and his strength;
seek his face always.
—1 CHRONICLES 16:11

I looked at the knitting project I held in my hands and gasped. "I can see the veins in my thumb."

The chitchat in our Thursday night knitting group halted as eight women processed my discovery. Those wonderful women had walked the journey through Better Than Ever with me and knew the significance of my unscripted comment. No, I had never seen veins in my thumb before. This was new and, come on, rather cool.

"Don't look at my face," one knitter said. "You'll see my wrinkles."

Oh, sweetheart, you have no idea. Since Better Than Ever, I can see wrinkles, moles, neck creases, and unbrushed hair. I plastered my hand on my head. *Does that mean you all know I'm overdue for a color job?*

Remember the cliché "Don't judge a book by its cover"? We know we shouldn't be self-conscious about body blemishes. No one's paying attention to how we look because they are too absorbed in their own stress-induced acne or menopausal facial hair to notice ours. *Judgments about physical attractiveness are silly*, the inner voice scolds.

Then a handsome guy enters the room and our hearts swoon. A slim and trim woman with a flawless face passes our table and our faces darken with envy. In that nanosecond, we shift our gaze from the inner character to the outer shell and set up our own grading system of someone's worth based on the physical.

It takes a season of isolation to make us reset our priorities about faces.

Your child is serving a two-year military deployment. You've been stuck in a rehab center recovering from hip surgery complications. Your parents bought a fifth wheel and headed to a warmer climate for the winter.

Then it's time for reunion. And you can hardly wait. *Don't bother with the hairbrush; I just want to see your face and hug your neck.* Those dear older faces lined with age and experience, and the younger ones in the bloom of youth. The sweet red-splotched face of a newborn grandchild. Precious friends sitting across the table, sharing their news and a cuppa.

Each uniquely marked face represents a person you know, respect, and love. Physical details no longer matter. If you can see a face, you are together. Close enough to touch a shoulder, grasp a hand, or hear their stories, sorrows, and sage advice. So close that someone else can't get between you.

In my seasons of separation, I worry that, as time goes on, I'll forget the faces of my important people and become complacent with the not seeing. That's what happened to the Israelites. Moses, the representative of God, went missing for five Sabbaths as he conferred with God on Mount Sinai. The people, eager to find a face replacement, looked for other gods (Exod. 32).

Moses, on the other hand, couldn't bear the thought of God's absence. When God proposed not going with the Israelites to the promised land because of their unfaithfulness, Moses became desperate. Like Henry Higgins in the Broadway musical *My Fair Lady*, who laments in the last scene that he's become accustomed to Eliza's face, Moses realized he couldn't function without God's presence. "Show me your glory," he pleaded in Exodus 33:18. God's response—that he would pass by a cleft in the rock where he would cover Moses with his hand—shows how up close and personal Moses wanted to get. He wanted the full view. For Moses, arm's length wouldn't do.

It won't do for God either.

You and I are encountering a God who wants to have face-to-face contact with the people he has created. That means close enough to know and understand him in detail, near enough to know what he is thinking. So close that other distractions won't get in the way.

That boggles my mind.

This holy, perfect God, mastermind of the universe—this glorious being who can create or destroy with one word—wants me near enough for companionship. Intimacy far grander than what a married couple of fifty years could possibly have.

Do I dare? Do you?

You see, that proximity to God will show us how holy, pure, and good he is. If we get that close, we'll understand his purposes, rationales, and passions. He'll let us watch him at work. We'll see him, but then it will become very apparent that he can see us. The blemishes and scars. The dirt and grime that tattle where we've been and what we've done. The haunted hurt in our eyes or the downcast shame for what we've become that we wish he didn't know already.

That's all right, my friend. He saw all that from afar, and he still invites you to get up close so you can see.

How do you get there?

> ## The more time you spend with God, the more you realize the depths of his love for you.

Start now to include him in your everyday activities. The more time you spend with God, the more you realize the depths of his love for you. As you discover his love, you'll want him to be part of every waking and sleeping moment. You will want to seek his face.

Make time in your schedule to ponder the intricacies of nature and ask yourself what it tells you about your God. Read his story through the pages of the Bible. Interact with like-minded people in whom his Spirit also dwells. Look for him in life experiences to discover how he uses the best and worst of times to bring about his greatest good. Imitate his ways so you become more like him.

The closer you get, the more you will reflect the light streaming from his face. That means you'll start looking like him. As Paul wrote, "And we all, who with unveiled faces contemplate the Lord's glory, are being transformed into his image with ever-increasing glory, which comes from the Lord, who is the Spirit" (2 Cor. 3:18).

And the world will forget your scars, wrinkles, and lines. Instead, they will see Jesus in you.

Lord, thank you for wanting a close relationship
with me despite my blemishes and imperfections.
Thank you for letting me see your face in all its
beauty. Show me how to see you more clearly.

SEEING WITH FRESH EYES

Pursue God today. Look for him throughout your day. Plan to share your discoveries with someone close to you.

30

Friends

I will instruct you and teach you in the
way you should go; I will counsel you with my
loving eye on you.
—PSALM 32:8

Visual loss can be isolating and lonely. Before Better Than Ever, if anyone stood beyond my six-foot bubble, they might as well not have been there. A friend could enter a room and I would have no clue. I had to wait for people to come to me.

As a pastor's wife, I live under self-made expectations that Sunday morning is my hour to greet as many people as possible and show concern about their past week and current needs. Don't take me wrong; I love nurturing my husband's flock. However, frustration used to fill my tummy every Sunday when I tried to peer past my visual limits to find the people I felt I needed to visit. I feared a newcomer or fringe member would feel rejected because I didn't speak to them. *No, I just didn't see you.*

One morning, I had a list of twelve people I needed to check in with for various reasons. Finding them would be impossible and I knew it. I would look like a lost child, with kindly intentioned people loudly announcing my dilemma: "Karen, who are you trying to find?" Since I'm slightly allergic to proclamations of my weaknesses, I cried out in desperation, *Oh, God, would you bring to me these people I need to see?*

After I reached home that day, I made a list of my morning's contacts. I had connected with every single person on my list, plus a few more. Conversations had gone deep, beyond peripheral greetings. I was exhausted but happy.

It worked at conferences too. Name tags are my nemesis, yet conferences are all about networking. *Oh, God, would you . . . ?* Same thing. Every person on my mental list. Every time.

Lord, who do you want me to see?

Then I felt ashamed. Wasn't I going about this backward? The second morning at one conference, I asked, *Lord, who do you want me to see?* The results were amazing. I met Anne, who worked for the same company I had done a freelance curriculum project for fifteen years before, and she and I shared how God had done marvelous things with that project. I had an hour-long talk with Susan, where we swiftly moved from conference matters to our personal lives and need for prayer.

All of us long to connect with the people who know us best and accept us as we are. Conversations are comfortable because we know what we can talk about. We beeline for seats by our friends so we can catch up on all the news.

What if that is not the path God wants you to take? What would happen if you prayed before you entered your church, the grocery store, the library, or the doorway of your home, *Lord, who do you want me to see?* When God directs our connections, we may discover moments that we didn't anticipate but that end up being far richer than the generic, everyday talk we expected. Because God is the best appointment coordinator.

After Better Than Ever, visual isolation was no longer an issue. I could see friends halfway across the room. How wonderful. Never again would I hang back, trying to distinguish friends by voices, familiar coats, or hair colors. Yet I began to miss those days when I had to depend on God. Now that I didn't need his help to connect with people, I wasn't coordinating with him about who to see that day as much as I used to. I longed for those sweet, intimate moments when my Lord and I worked together to nurture his people.

Nothing had changed on his end; why did anything have to change on mine? Why couldn't I still ask him, *Who do* you *want me to see?* The change came in that now I had a choice. Should I visit with the people I could see, or was I willing to trust God with his contact list to see who he wanted me to see?

When you and I choose to depend on God for what we think we can do by ourselves, he will take us in directions we never considered possible. And, oh, it is sweet.

I decided to look for those who, like me before Better Than Ever, were waiting to be seen. Like the ninety-three-year-old woman who sat in a chair behind the back row in our church's worship service and didn't move for the next hour, even to greet people, because walking from the parking lot to the sanctuary took all her energy. The two elderly women whose dizzy spells kept them from moving as fast as the rest of us. Or the one standing alone whose shyness created another kind of six-foot barrier.

I took my search outside the doors of the church and into a local store. There was the woman in an electric cart who couldn't reach beyond the third shelf. The wiggling child seated in the cart in front of me in the checkout line. The store cashier whose methodical, slow movements and shadowed eyes indicated she didn't feel well and was having a bad day.

Even on days when we are stuck at home, hungering for human contact and composing lists of those we want to hug when we see them next, the question, the prayer, is still valid. *Lord, this day, who do* you *want me to see?*

Some days, the Lord might have ready a list of twelve people. Other times, his answer may come in a single word: *Me.*

For he longs to be our best friend and catch up on the news of our lives too.

Lord, who do you want me to see today? Turn me around, face me in the direction you want me to go, and help me connect.

SEEING WITH FRESH EYES

What doorways will you enter today? Who do you plan to see? Turn your contact list over to God and ask, "Lord, in this place, who do you want me to see today?"

31

Shopping Carts

*You will be enriched in every way so that you can
be generous on every occasion, and through us
your generosity will result in thanksgiving to God.*
—2 CORINTHIANS 9:11

*M*y husband considered it a good day when I met him at a super-store exit with a smile instead of tears. That meant two things: I found bargains, and I probably ran into only one cart this trip.

At times I wondered why any store management allowed me through their doors. With no side vision or depth perception, judging distances between me and other customers' carts was dicey. I often passed off my clumsiness with a joke, telling other shoppers I didn't have a driver's license. We would exchange smiles, but I withered with embarrassment.

I longed to care for my family on my own, but over the years, shopping caused more frustration than joy. With the nearest store often fifteen miles from my home, I went only when someone could drive me. I stuck to a list of basic items and preferred smaller, familiar stores. Unable to see detail, I was clueless about the existence of many products. If I wanted something out of the ordinary, I had to either ask—if

I could find a clerk—or do without. Out-of-sight, out-of-mind products made for quicker shopping trips, lower food bills, and one trying-to-be-content mama.

Now, with Better Than Ever, shopping trips lengthened as I lingered over aisle signs, endcaps, and stand-alone displays. My receipt totals crept upward because I was discovering all these wonderful products and irresistible deals.

One day, my delight over bargains loaded my cart. "I don't know why I bought all this," I told my more than patient husband, who didn't expect any explanation. I had filled my basket with cans of pumpkin, cartons of chicken broth, a whole chicken, and two pounds of deli ham. Whatever was I thinking? We don't even use processed broth.

The next day, we heard about two families who could use a good home-cooked meal. An unwed new mother was on her way home with her baby. Another mama of five children was seriously ill in the hospital. Our community of believers is a generous, compassionate group, shown by how they provided meals for us after my surgery. I love to cook, and I'd wanted to return the blessing, but not being able to drive myself to the store often kept me from cooking for others like I wanted. Only a few days before this last shopping trip, I had cried to the Lord, *I want to love my neighbors with food gifts. Will you help me serve in love?*

This time, I had all I needed to make a large pot of chicken and noodles, and plates of cookies for both families.

God will supply whatever you need to do the work he calls you to do.

God will supply whatever you need to do the work he calls you to do. Some days, he will stock your shelves with an extra abundance, in ways that may not make sense to you at the moment. But he knows your future and the good works he has planned for you (Eph. 2:10).

After all, if you have agreed to make Jesus Christ Lord of your life, you are now in partnership with the Holy Spirit. You've had a makeover in your DNA, and the Spirit of God is hardwired into your spirit. In practical terms, that means you and I will begin acting in ways that are part of his plan, even though we may not know the reasons beforehand. As we live and move and have our being in him (Acts 17:28), we will make choices that may seem out of the ordinary for us but are in full sync with the Spirit who lives within us.

It gives me tingles.

Is there something you've wanted to do for Jesus but you feel frustrated by the obstacles? Ask the Lord to provide so you can do the job he has for you. Then be attentive to those little Holy Spirit nudges that lead you to take steps toward that goal.

When you ask for God's direction, he will provide. He'll whisper an action plan that will bring about his good purposes, asking you to trust him with the big-picture details. Your responsibility and privilege is to listen to that still, small voice and reach for what he puts within your line of vision, even if it seems out of the ordinary at the time.

Like cartons of chicken broth in overflowing grocery carts.

Thank you, Lord, for providing all I need to be generous on every occasion. I want to listen and follow better, trusting you'll provide what I need to extend your love to others who need your help too.

SEEING WITH FRESH EYES

Look through the extras in your pantry, bookshelf, or clothes closet. How might the Lord want you to use what you have to bless others?

32

Family Doctor

*The one who is the true light, who gives light to
everyone, was coming into the world.*
—JOHN 1:9 (NLT)

Eager to test the limits of my improved vision, I joined our church's
bell choir that performed at the annual Christmas Eve service. I
asked for what I thought would be the easiest position, the three bells
at the top of the two-octave range. The high G I held was the opening
note of "Joy to the World," the first song on the roster. If I missed my
entrance, everyone would know. I renewed my resolve. Surely I could
see the conductor's cue.

During practice I did fine. At the Christmas Eve service, I almost
blew it—not because I couldn't see but because of what I could see.
More specifically, *who* I could see.

Our two long tables of bells linked the entrance hallway with the
back of the darkened sanctuary. Worshippers flowed around our tables
before they entered the auditorium to find seats. I felt torn between
concentrating on performance prep and greeting people as they passed
my end of the table.

As I grasped my bells, ready for the opening cue, I saw him.

I wasn't expecting him to be there. He occasionally attended special programs at our church with his mother and brothers, who were members. Then there was the matter of street clothes. You know how it is—it's hard to recognize people when they are out of their element. This guy didn't have a stethoscope wrapped around his neck.

He was my primary care doctor, our family doctor.

Recognition alone almost made me drop my bell. I wasn't used to visually identifying anyone, a social faux pas over which I had much private embarrassment. But that night, I knew. It was him.

A second realization made me consider abandoning my bells altogether. I hadn't seen him since—why, since my pre-op physical exam before the Better Than Ever surgery. No colds, sinus infections, or injuries had required a visit to his office. He didn't know my news.

Wait. Stop the program. Doctor, I have something to tell you. Wouldn't he want to know that, for once, a patient got better instead of worse? That one patient did more than recover to status quo?

He slipped into the dark sanctuary, and my hand gripped my high G bell as I put equal force into keeping my mouth closed. I wanted to shout, "I can see you now." As I peered into the dim auditorium, strewn with miniature Christmas lights, evergreen wreaths, and the backlit cross of Christ, the joy of the miracle washed over me like a Christmas Eve snow shower. *Oh, God, thank you that I can see. What did I ever do to deserve this special gift?* Who needed packages tied up with string? I could see—that was the best gift this girl could ever get for Christmas.

Not quite.

In an isolated pasture outside the town of Bethlehem, shepherds watched over their flocks, alert for intruders. They didn't expect to see the glorious visitor who stood among them. Brawny men, experienced at warding off bears, wolves, and lions, trembled in fear. Reassuring them, the angel delivered his good news: *A Savior is born. He is Christ the Lord.* (See Luke 2:11.)

Those shepherds left their sheep, found the baby Jesus, worshipped, and then did what I wanted to do. They told everyone they met. It was news worth sharing, the best of news, the kind that releases the deepest of joy.

It's no wonder the shepherds were busting to tell what they knew. Jewish born and bred, they'd heard all their lives about the promise God had disclosed through his prophet Isaiah: "The people walking in darkness have seen a great light; on those living in the land of deep darkness, a light has dawned" (Isa. 9:2). They recognized the long-awaited moment had come. God showed up, intent on keeping his promise.

Light has dawned. The dark night of waiting is over. You are not stuck any longer. You can see the way out of your confusion and hope-lessness. You don't have to feel defeated, helpless, or afraid ever again. Life no longer has to be resigned as a fatalistic mess.

Someone had to be the source of that light, someone who cared enough to make your path visible. That person is Jesus. God has not abandoned us. He didn't forget about us. He has not given up on his wayward world. He loves us all enough to provide a way back to rela-tionship with himself. He kept all those promises he made centuries before.

God came into the world to share our mess and do what only he could do to fix it. That is reason enough for joy.

That's what the birth of Jesus signifies. God came into the world to share our mess and do what only he could do to fix it. That is reason enough for joy. Joy far greater than a little bit of sight improvement in the middle of life. And when you and I get that fresh look at our world through the light Jesus sheds, life will be forever better rather than worse.

When the shepherds investigated what the angel told them, they found it was true, got really excited, and blabbed what they'd seen and heard to anyone who would listen. They could not contain their exhilaration.

When you have joy over something wonderful, you can't hold it back. The emotion spills out, unabashed, through breathless excitement and shining faces. And the birth of Jesus is something worth getting excited about. Christians, of all people, should celebrate Christmas well, for we have much to celebrate. *Look what God has done.*

I lifted my smallest bell and rang its note with one small word proclaiming the news. Joy!

Joy to the world, the Lord has come.

> *Lord, the calendar date of Christmas cannot begin
> to contain my joy for the coming of your Son. Help
> me cultivate an ever-growing excitement every
> day for the great thing you did when you brought
> your light into the darkness of our world.*

SEEING WITH FRESH EYES

Take a fresh look at how Jesus entered your life and the difference he has made. How can you respond with joy for what he has done for you?

33

Driver's License

Then Jesus told his disciples a parable
to show them that they should always pray
and not give up.
—LUKE 18:1

My eyes leaked tears for two days after my daughter, Christine, said she was eligible to get a driver's license.

My emotions were not the normal "clear the road" misgivings of a parent with a fifteen-year-old wannabe driver. They were happy tears of a mother who had accepted long before that her twenty-six-year-old daughter would never drive. It was beyond impossible, completely out of the question, never open for discussion. Now, God privileged our family to see an answer, and the answer was not *No.*

As parents, Jack and I tried to imprint a can-do spirit in our girls, teaching them to not accept the opinions of naysayers. Yet reality says there are certain things we simply cannot do. Advanced medical technology gave Christine better vision than I had, but driving a car was the one activity all of us accepted she would never do. So we taught her instead to fashion life choices around finding other ways to get around. The absence of a driver's license didn't have to keep her stuck at home.

Public transportation, taxi services, and (gulp) asking for rides from friends. Investing in good shoes because walking would be part of her lifestyle. *Focus on what you can do; not what you can't. And if you own a bike, best not to tell your mother about it.*

God had different ideas.

When a specialist corrected her refraction to 20/50, he leaned back in his chair. "Have you considered driving?"

No. Absolutely not.

Imagine believing all your life that you are prohibited from doing something. You're not good enough. You don't have the skill set. You weren't born into the right socioeconomic class. Your past sins will never let you reach the level of grace you crave. In two words, *you can't.*

Or maybe you've given up on someone else. They'll never become a believer, relinquish that nasty addiction, wiggle free from that chain-choking sin. "They are what they are," I've heard defeated voices say. "They'll never change."

When we give up on others, aren't we saying that God's grace is not capable of transforming lives? Have you known someone whose life has been altered by the love of Christ? If it is possible for them, then isn't it equally conceivable for the one you know?

And then God tells you, *You can. They can.* Hope is born. A pinprick of light shines into the certainty of darkness. The emotions run deep as your mind races with the ramifications of your newfound freedoms.

God is God. Impossible doesn't fit with his nature.

All things are possible. God is God. Impossible doesn't fit with his nature. If he can part the Red Sea, give sight to a blind man, make the sun stand still, and raise his Son from death to life, he can do anything. *Anything.* Even those things we don't dare to dream in the deepest of sleep. And before we question whether he will, resigning ourselves to a probable won't, did we ask? Seek? Try? Have we persisted? Or have we taken a first-time setback as a final no?

Jesus once told a parable about a feisty, brash widow who wouldn't take no for an answer (Luke 18:1–8). First-century Jewish culture said a widow had no legal recourse. If her husband died, their property was deeded to his inheritor, either a son or her late husband's brother. Society could easily take advantage of the widow and leave her destitute. Yes, Old Testament law provided for widows, but corrupt men could hold seats of judgment and adversaries could be powerful and ruthless. I wonder if the widow in Jesus's story ever caved to thinking her situation was permanent. Yet she persisted and finally got what she needed, not because the judge had a change of heart but because she wore him down.

Jesus calls his followers to persist too. After all, God is far more dependable, consistent, and loving than a corrupt judge.

Don't get me wrong. Learning to drive was not easy for Christine. Because she had lived for years with the "I can't" of driving, Christine had no concept of road rules or knowledge about the inner workings of a car. After a year of lessons with a very patient instructor, she still went through more attempts at the driver's test than she cared to remember or admit to her parents. After each failed exam, she fought the temptation to cave. But like the widow in Jesus's story, she persisted.

She kept trying because she recognized God had given her a gift she had long believed she would never have. "To capitulate would be to devalue the gift," she told me. She wrote later in her journal, "If God's the one giving this, then how would he be glorified if I quit?"

Let's redefine the word *impossible* as "I'm Possible." The great I AM, Jehovah God, can make it happen. And when the impossible happens, all who watch our resilient pursuit will know this could have only occurred by the power of God.

Jesus connects persistence with faith at the end of his parable when he says, "When the Son of Man comes, will he find faith on the earth?" (Luke 18:8). That kind of faith is the confident belief that God can do anything, even those things beyond the realm of possibility. Giving up, on the other hand, releases our grip on that belief that God is God and can do anything. Yes, we may never reach the level of impossible we hope for. It may not come on our timetable. But when we hold unswervingly to God's ability to bring about his good will, we find hope for the future and accept his best for the moment.

Don't give up. Keep trying. Let Jesus find your resilient faith upon the earth. Prove your confidence in him by persistently pursuing what you believe God has called you to do. If he is in it, it will happen in his way and his time.

Push those doubts away that say you can't. Keep believing that God can do anything. I know he can. Our family saw him do it. And you've probably seen him do it too. No matter where you've been, no matter what others have said, you can be all that God calls you to be.

Lord, forgive me for the times I've resigned myself
to contentment with the status quo. Right now,
I want to persist in prayer for an impossible
situation in my life.

SEEING WITH FRESH EYES

What do you want to accomplish for God? Pray, plan, persist, and pray some more. God loves you so much. He's in your court and he wants what is best for you.

34

Driver's Seat

I will lead the blind by ways they have not known,
along unfamiliar paths I will guide them; I will turn
the darkness into light before them and make the
rough places smooth. These are the things I will
do; I will not forsake them.
—ISAIAH 42:16

Her first time behind the wheel, Christine backed her sister's car out of the driveway and inched the car down the street, Katherine coaching her from the passenger's seat.

Let me be honest. This was one scene I did not see. I couldn't watch. I was too chicken. When I saw Christine close the driver's door, I fled into the house. Whatever had I agreed to?

They took off for a country road to give her experience at higher speeds. They sent me a video with her looking at the camera. *Would you please keep your eyes on the road?*

A quick peek at her driving down the street filled me with awe. My heart of gratitude competed with my churning stomach. This driving thing was finally happening. But could she really do this? Would I see the car and two daughters return all in one piece?

I texted my friend Gloria. "Christine is driving. Is it all right to have a knot in my tummy?"

I chided myself. What was the worst that could happen? A car wreck? Death? Both my girls knew Jesus. Death meant heaven. I couldn't deny them that. The worst for a mother, I think, is seeing your child hurt, physically or emotionally. I can't handle watching my children suffer even though I of all people know that suffering cultivates strength. I'm the mom who would go through more eye surgery if it kept my baby from feeling pain. My heart wrenched whenever my girls brought home a failing grade. Not because of disappointment in them. I couldn't bear to witness their disappointment in themselves.

Watching our children, or our children in the faith, falter when they leap toward new achievements is never easy. Breath catches in our throat as we wait for that instant they realize they are in free fall and we are too far away to catch them. It's then that we define faith by our ability to be still and stay put. We painfully recognize how much we need to trust the God who is there to catch them.

Nothing will happen to them that he doesn't already know about. As parents and mentors, we do our part to prepare and guide, and then our responsibility is to stand aside and let God unfurl his plan for their best. The God who gave Christine this chance to drive also had the power to protect and lead her through the learning curve.

But I feel so out of control.

I don't know about you, but I find it fairly easy to believe God could protect my child from physical harm. I believe it because I want to believe it. It's a lot harder to believe that God could do great and awesome things with and through my children's lives when they enter seasons of physical suffering, heartache, or sickness. That just like he did for me, God can and will, if they allow him to, strengthen their spiritual sight to see him Better Than Ever through whatever circumstances they encounter.

Who did I trust? I trusted my daughters. I knew they were responsible adults. Christine's look away from the road at the camera was only three seconds. *But I don't trust other drivers*, I wanted to cry out.

I worried that Christine wouldn't react well to any new challenge and that her older sister would get impatient. I forgot to put God in the equation of the driving lesson's success.

Until Gloria reminded me.

She texted back, "A little knot is allowed. They will be all right. Remember, they are God's girls first and he is in the car now."

God is in the car. He knows everything about my girls. Their strengths, their weaknesses, their present moment, and their future. He will give them the wisdom they need when they ask. He is with them in whatever they face—just as he has been with me. Even if the worst happened, God will still be there, caring, loving, nurturing, and protecting them from anything the devil dares to throw at them.

God cares for those you love more than you do.

God cares for those you love more than you do. He is ever present with them when your reach falls short. God calls you and me to let go so they can realize their need to catch hold of his hand and trust him for themselves.

Lord God, I believe in you, but my unbelief shows
up when I need to rise above my circumstances
and trust in you as Lord of the moment. Thank you
for your patience and love as I learn to relinquish
those I love into your care.

SEEING WITH FRESH EYES

Who under your watch seems to be faltering? Their current circumstances do not define the end result of their success. Put your person in God's hands and ask him to do his best work in them.

35

Walmart Signs

For you were once darkness, but now you are light
in the Lord. Live as children of light.
—EPHESIANS 5:8

*J*ack and I stood in a Walmart checkout line. After I placed our purchases on the counter, I raised my head and looked around. I poked my husband. "Walmart has signs on the wall for the various departments." My finger pointed out the signs as I mouthed the words: Customer Service, Restrooms, Optical, Produce . . .

He shrugged and pulled out his debit card.

I gawked. So that's how people find items in department stores.

Me? I guess. If I see a bottle of vitamins, I must be in the pharmacy. I memorize. Produce is on the right as soon as you walk in the right side of the store. No, wait, it's different in the Walmart the next town over. Don't you dare rearrange your store aisles: I just got this figured out.

Now I could see signs. How convenient. I moved to the bag carousel to help load our purchases, but continued my open-mouthed and wide-eyed exploration.

Another clerk approached me. "May I help you?" Her voice sounded hesitant and concerned.

Without thinking, I answered, "No, thanks, I'm just reading signs." I'm certain she took a step back. I suppose it wasn't every day she encountered middle-aged customers who got excited about reading signs. *You need a life,* she probably mouthed.

Honey, you got off easy, my mental telepathy shot back. *I'm restraining myself from grabbing your collar and shouting, "I can see!"*

My husband was amused. I was only slightly fazed. "You can't take me anywhere, can you?" I quipped. I was too excited to blush about my zany, slightly neurotic behavior.

One thought tempered my delight. Would I be as unconcerned with others' reactions if I expressed excitement about my relationship with Jesus? Could joy over God's gracious choice to forgive and remove my sin and guilt shroud my fear of what others might think? Could my trust in God become so hardwired into my character that I'm hardly aware of how I'm standing out in stark contrast to the rest of the world—as different, as the Bible challenges us, as light is to dark?

Christians are different people. In a world filled with darkness, we're called children of light. Yet this contrast needs to come from the inside out. If we merely go through the motions of our faith, it's an act, a put-on that could so easily be marred by a double standard. Claiming a biblical worldview isn't enough either, for our watching audience will consider our intellectual arguments irrelevant and contentious if they aren't supported by our lifestyle.

Those observing your faith want authenticity.

Those observing your faith want authenticity. They want proof that this Jesus thing is for real and can make a difference right here, right now. When you allow Christ to redesign your behavior into his likeness, to recode the DNA of your character, that's when the world will sit up, take notice, and want what you have.

Your behavior will change, not because you have to but because you want to. Like my uninhibited reaction to my new eyesight, you'll respond in delight to God's incredible gift and how his forgiveness has released you from guilt's prison. Death becomes no longer an obstacle or a dead end, but a stepping-stone to the beginning of eternity. Your experience of God's love for you will compel you to love others, regardless of what they do, how they act, or how they react to your unexpected concern for them. You've discovered God's patience with you, so in gratitude, and through his power, you'll be more patient with the shortcomings of the person next to you.

When *different* becomes a natural way of life, we will hear comments like these:

"I like coming to your house. I feel peace here."

"You seem like you are people of joy."

"How can you keep loving your ex-spouse like that? I'd never be able to be a caregiver for my ex."

"You are the soul of patience."

Jesus told the disciples right before his death that our brand of unconditional love would mark us as believers (John 13:35). In that same talk, he told them that bearing fruit is an identification tag of belief that brings the Father glory (15:16). What fruit or results did Jesus mean? The fruit of the Spirit outlined in Galatians—love, joy, peace, patience, kindness, goodness, faithfulness, gentleness, and self-control—are all character traits, not external rituals or philosophies. We can't program or playact character traits. As our awareness of the great and awesome thing Jesus did for us grows, gratitude will nourish our character change, and the world will take note.

If you claim to be a follower of Christ, he calls you to be noticeably different: a crazy, confusing, obnoxious, and alluring kind of different. Some in your watching audience won't get it and may question your motives and your sanity. That's because your lifestyle will catch them off guard. It's not part of their playlist. Yet, when we live the changed life of Christ in addition to proclaiming the gospel message, there will be those who inwardly long for what we have.

So don't hide your excitement over the beauty of creation or your delight over what you see God doing. Don't withhold your compassion in showing mercy to others, and be free to disclose the motive behind your actions—*Jesus has done this for me.* Let wonder, gratitude, and kindness spill out of you. As Jesus directed, shine your light (Matt. 5:16). You might get some initial kickback, but ultimately your authenticity will attract more than repel.

Be distinct. Make them wonder.

> *Lord, fill me with the joy of my salvation so much*
> *that it wraps around every part of my character*
> *and shines through in ways that compel those*
> *around me to consider who you are.*

SEEING WITH FRESH EYES

What excites you about your relationship with God? Answered prayers, the grandeur of creation, the unity you experience in a group of believers? Don't be afraid to share your excitement with unbelievers and strangers. It might start some interesting conversations.

36

Shuttle Driver

My mouth is filled with your praise, declaring your
splendor all day long.
—PSALM 71:8

The memo from the conference director told Laura, the shuttle driver, that her early-arrival pickup for the conference was a visually impaired woman. True to protocol, Laura and I exchanged information about where to meet in the airport and descriptions of our clothes and my carry-on bag. Her last-minute text told me she was wearing black-and-white polka dots.

She hit Send and then laughed at herself. Her pickup was visually impaired; how would she see polka dots?

Laura's embarrassment peaked when she called out to me at the airport. Her eyes grew round as she surveyed me from top to toe. "Karen?" Her hand flew to her mouth. "I'm sorry. I didn't recognize you. I thought you would be holding a white cane."

My instant comeback flew out of my mouth before my sensible brain could stop it. "Oh, I threw away my white cane two years ago."

If Laura's eyes could open any farther, they did. She didn't need to say, "What?" Her face said it all.

"I guess I have a story to tell," I said as we headed to baggage claim.

There in that public airport, while we waited for my luggage, I told the story of Better Than Ever. After the glazed look of the Walmart employee, I didn't expect an emotional reaction, but Laura lifted her hand to her face, this time to wipe tears. And all the way from the airport to the conference center, we shared worship of a God who redeems people and situations, and who brings good out of bad because he's madly, lavishly in love with us.

Laura invited me to join the staff and early-arriving faculty for a box supper. As we sat down, the conference director asked if all had gone well at the airport pickup. "Karen," Laura said, "tell your story." So now I had the opportunity to share Better Than Ever with an instant audience of fifteen people. For the rest of the conference, people kept approaching me. "I was there when you told your story." Their shining faces revealed their reactions.

This wasn't the only time someone has prompted me to share the Better Than Ever story. Friends have introduced me to their friends with, "Karen, tell what happened to you." Laura's emotional response showed I had a story to tell and I didn't need to be shy about sharing it. Jack has learned to step back and let me grab moments to tell perfect strangers why I'm particularly enamored with simple things like birds' nests and robins pecking in dew-kissed grass.

I've come a long way from wanting to grab my family doctor by his coat collar. I've learned to watch for openings and keep the story to a tight two or three sentences. I look for any life prompt: motorcycles, sunsets, museum tours, and, yes, store signs. I sculpt the story to make it appealing, tantalizing, and God-glorifying. With each telling, I grow in my boldness and skill to weave in the God factor. Through practice, I've learned my audience's receptivity depends largely on my first line and my positive attitude in the telling.

What's your story? You don't think you have one? You do. It doesn't have to be a sensational salvation account. Nor does it have to be only the moment that began your walk with Jesus. Simply tell what God has done for you. It can be anything from healing of cancer to saving your marriage, dealing with a wayward child, the time someone left a bag of groceries on your doorstep when, unknown to them, you were down to your last dollar, or the endurance God granted you to make it through a season of suffering. If an observer of your crisis asks, "Aren't you scared?" you can say, "No, not really" or "Yes, but then . . ." and tell how God gives you hope that moves you past the fear.

The chance to tell our redemption story may come when we least expect it. Our job is simple: be ready, grab the moment, and take the time to tell it. The apostle Peter wrote, "Always be prepared to give an answer to everyone who asks you to give the reason for the hope that you have. But do this with gentleness and respect" (1 Peter 3:15). Did you catch that? *Always* be prepared. That means we can't stick our testimony into a one-size-fits-all plan for the telling. Chances to tell our stories are infinite and infinitely varied. With God's help, we can always be ready, no matter the circumstances.

When we shape our story in winsome ways that define hope and create a picture of joy and gratitude without belaboring the point, our audience will notice. They'll appreciate our respect for their time and how we present our beliefs without clobbering them over the head with salvation facts. Instead, we're simply saying, "This is what God has done for me." They'll listen, wish for more, and tell their friends, "You have to hear this story."

Identify the role God has played in your life events.

How can you prepare for unexpected moments? Know your story. Identify the role God has played in your life events. Be so aware of his part and grateful for what he has done that the story flows naturally. Then pray at each day's beginning, *Lord, who needs to hear my story today?* Ask God to put words in your mouth that today's audience needs to hear.

Watch out. He's ingenious, that God of ours. He might give you a story starter like, "I threw away my white cane two years ago."

Lord, show me the story you want me to tell that
will bring you glory and draw others to your
redemptive love.

SEEING WITH FRESH EYES

To be able to tell a story means you must know your story. What specific things has God done for you? Block out time today to make a list. What's your opening line to your story?

37

Tom and Shirley

He has delivered us from such a deadly peril,
and he will deliver us again. On him we have
set our hope that he will continue to deliver us,
as you help us by your prayers. Then many will
give thanks on our behalf for the gracious favor
granted us in answer to the prayers of many.
—2 CORINTHIANS 1:10–11

I met Tom and his wife, Shirley, at a memorial service for a church member. I stood in a gathering area, greeting people as they arrived. Tom's handshake had a familiarity that puzzled me. "I don't think we've met," I said.

"But I know you." His smile equaled the warmth of his handclasp. He moved his hand to my shoulder as if in blessing. "We know about your eyesight. How have you been since surgery?" He paused and added the final personal touch of grace. "We've been praying for you."

I made the connection. Tom's sister-in-law lived in our small town. Awkwardness turned into deep emotion. A mere thank-you wouldn't begin to cover my gratitude. Strangers who had heard about my sight loss had stopped to pray for me, not with a one-time, fix-it-and-forget-it mindset, but with ongoing intentionality. They cared enough to ask about the outcome. *Oh, let me tell you what God has done.*

We are not alone. None of us. We are in this life thing together. God established the church so believers could stand united and lift up each other. Your sorrow is my sorrow; your joy, my joy. Your success is sweetness to my soul, and you feel the pain of my failure. We grip hands, finding that struggle is eased in the sharing. That's the comfort of Christian partnership.

At times, my prayer list has grown long with people I didn't personally know, and I've wondered if I'm doing any good by mouthing monotonous prayers for healing, peace, and comfort. Yet, when I was the recipient, the prayers of this unknown friend moved me to that place of emotion beyond words and tears.

There's something mystical about intercessory prayer. Why do people speak of the power of prayer or say, "Prayer works"? Prayer is powerful because it accomplishes far more than God's answer to our petitions. Prayer links believers together, for it combines my spirit with the spirits of others and melds them with the Spirit of God. The three parts are all in agreement of what we would like to see happen. We stand, hands clasped, joined with one intention in the presence of God. We wonder if we should take off our shoes, for surely the ground beneath our feet is holy. No other bond on earth can be so strong.

Prayer for someone else in the name of Jesus is a kind of grace, an unconditional love. It looks at the need, not whether the person deserves God's generosity. Poor choices that caused the mess fade to the background. Someone has a need, and those who pray know the one who can help best. The motivation to pray is an extension of compassion, a longing for life to be better no matter who needs it or what they've done that might label them as unworthy. Prayer for another becomes a beautiful, living-out-loud example of the grace God showed us in Jesus's death on the cross on our behalf.

Prayer confirms our shared admission that we are dependent on God and helpless without him. Our requests confess our spiritual bankruptcy to solve problems on our own. Asking the Lord for his divine intervention articulates our trust in the God who has the authority and interest to do what we cannot do.

Prayer proclaims God's power to a watching world. If no one knows about the need for prayer, they won't know how God answers. But when word spreads and God's people are invited to pray specifically and publicly for something, then, when God answers, all those who prayed and everyone else who overhears will rejoice in God's goodness. Tom, Shirley, and others in the room heard me say, "Let me tell you what God has done."

News about my gift of sight spread beyond that room and past that morning. Imagine the scenario. A church in a rural town hears about a legally blind pastor's wife in another isolated town, and she is losing what precious little vision she has. They pray and ask others to pray. The unthinkable happens. Not only does God carry the woman through surgery; he gives her better vision than she has ever had in her life.

Consider the excitement of the messenger: "Remember that woman I asked you to pray for? Let me tell what God has done." Strangers will tell strangers the story: "I heard about this legally blind woman in her midfifties whose sight has doubled after a random surgery." And the story spreads, far beyond the boundaries of either rural community.

It started because people chose to pray for someone they knew only through another.

> As Christ followers, we have our marching orders: pray, hope, and tell—so the world may know what God has done.

The world watches the concern believers have for each other, the confidence they place in the hope they say they have, and their reaction when God delivers. As Christ followers, we have our marching orders: pray, hope, and tell—so the world may know what God has done.

Lord, I know of someone who needs your help.
Would you do great and mighty things for them so
the people in their circle of influence can see what
you can do?

SEEING WITH FRESH EYES

Have you recently seen a prayer request for someone you don't know personally? Pause right now and pray for them. Then find a way to check for an update and publicly praise God for what he has done.

38

Transformed People

And we all, who with unveiled faces contemplate
the Lord's glory, are being transformed into his
image with ever-increasing glory, which comes
from the Lord, who is the Spirit.
—2 CORINTHIANS 3:18

*E*nthralled with my new eyesight, I couldn't see past the end of my own excitement.

I thought I was cute. I would greet friends with, "It's so good to *see* you." I meant what I said. What a thrill to see the finer details that told me who friends were and how they felt that day. Like a child who has just learned to read, I was fascinated with my newfound world: squirrels, street signs, and color-etched sunsets. I babbled with excitement to anyone who would listen.

My joyful greeting brought smiles to most faces. "I imagine it is," they said. Then Frank did the unpredictable and shifted my sights to the unseen. Gripping my hand, his voice rattled with emotion: "It's good to be seen."

Frank could say that. A three-time stroke victim, Frank should have been dead or at the very least tucked into a wheelchair in a full-care facility. But Frank walked and talked and rejoiced over the renewal of his driver's license. He knew the joy of reclaimed life. His presence at church functions was not a right or a choice but a precious privilege.

The truth dawned. I was not the only one who had received the grace of renewal. Aware I'd been shortsighted in thinking solely about my own miracle, I asked God to open my eyes to see who else treasured the gift of being seen.

The list was long. I saw transformed people all around me who, like Frank, had felt God's presence in the valley of the shadow of death and rejoiced in the privilege of life.

Susie, a three-time cancer survivor, still living, working, and joy-filled.

Vernie, the church elder whose love for gathering with God's people intensified after a life-threatening heart attack and its ensuing recovery had forced him to stay away.

Connie, who, after five hip surgeries and a broken arm, was convinced she could not have made it through those three horrible years without God's help.

Then there were those who experienced God's mercy and grace in the remaking of their inner spirits.

The hard-living truck driver who met Christ midlife and said with utter conviction about Christ's ability to forgive, "I get it."

The store clerk who, after years of hard living and bad choices, encountered Christ and moved to our small town to start again. Her joy greeted each customer at the grocery store and her servant's heart overflowed with kindness to her neighbors.

And me. Bound by rules and regs, despairing of my inadequacies, I got a bright look at the meaning of grace in a seminary classroom. What to some may have been dry theology became life-giving water, for I realized God could forgive my sin only through the voluntary death of his Son and not by anything I did to earn his approval. In that moment, I truly began to see.

Each one of us so grateful for what we had gained because we had seen God alter our character, behavior, and life situations in ways only he could do.

> ## God's transformation happens to *all* who surrender their weaknesses, their strengths, and their pain to his remaking.

The best part is that God's transformation happens to *all* who surrender their weaknesses, their strengths, and their pain to his remaking. Like a child who grows up to look just like her mother, we grow into the likeness of our heavenly Father as we mature in our faith. We know—oh yes, we know—that God's power is real, because we've seen it.

When you compare what you've become to what you used to be, joyful gratitude will shine as strong as a beacon on a rock-strewn shoreline. You can't miss it. It shouts of second chances, restorations, and rescues. If you can't initially see it, ask God to give you a fresh look at what he sees within the deep recesses of your character. I think you'll find that you are far from what you can be, yet so much further from what you used to be.

Let the sight of what more you can become spur you on toward greater life change, for life can be so much more than it is, and you've already experienced some of that. You don't have to make those changes all by yourself to get God's approval. If you have signed the contract that accepts God's plan for your salvation, your Lord has rolled up his divine sleeves and started the work of transforming you into his likeness. You are who you are today because God has done a great thing for you and within you.

Just as he has done for those who join you in worshipping the Christ. We need to listen to the stories of those who stand beside us, who find it good to be seen because they know God has brought them to where they are.

Perhaps you've hit a road bump of discouragement. You wonder if it's possible to be any better than you are. You don't have a clue of how to get there from here. Try this. Sit beside an older saint of God. Ask them to share with you their recollections about their faith journey. Find someone who has been through the crucible of suffering and ask how they were able to maintain their faith in a loving God. Ask how God provided and how they knew God was walking with them. Ask how God has helped them be stronger for the struggle.

The next time your community of believers gathers, look at those who surround you. Others have a story to tell too, how God has rescued them, reclaimed them, and given them gifts they don't deserve and strength beyond what is normal for them. God created and is re-creating them, as well as you, into his likeness.

Then turn to the person next to you and say with new understanding, "It's so good to *see* you." Because it is good to see and good to be seen.

Lord, I revel in the joy of rebirth and restoration.
Thank you for giving me new chances to live within
the sphere of your glory. It is good to be seen
because of what you have done within me.

SEEING WITH FRESH EYES

Reflect on the changes you've seen in your life over the past ten years. How has God changed you to be more like him?

39

McDonald's Clerk

*But blessed are your eyes because they see, and
your ears because they hear.*
—MATTHEW 13:16

Getting weird reactions to my strange behavior of staring at business signs was becoming the norm. No problem for me. One more chance to tell the story. Bless his heart, Jack would stand back and let me. Then he would patiently prop up my burst enthusiasm when my listeners didn't react how I thought they would.

As I waited for a McDonald's cashier to fill my coffee order, I stared at the overhead menu, trying to make out words.

"Can I get you something else?" the polite young man asked.

"Oh no, I'm just trying to read the sign." By now, I'd realized the importance of explaining my atypical behavior. "I had eye surgery several months ago that gave me better vision than I've ever had before, and I'm having so much fun exploring what I can now see."

He perked up. A good sign. "Oh. Did you have LASIK surgery?"

"No." I paused. "I had a torn retina and other issues from childhood that . . ." I could see well enough to know his gaze had slid to the customer behind me. I trailed off, picked up my coffee, and found my husband, who had already claimed a table.

The clerk didn't get it. He didn't get it because all he knew was LASIK surgery.

How could I describe my complicated eye disorder in thirty seconds or less to help this stranger understand the significance of that sight-giving surgery? Why couldn't he be like my shuttle driver and have tears running down his cheeks within thirty seconds of the telling?

Because it wasn't the time or place, and he wasn't ready. He was busy and I was infringing on his work schedule.

It would be lovely if our unbelieving friends and random contacts were instantly responsive to our joyful retellings of what God has done in our lives. Sadly, it's not that straightforward.

Maybe you've seen these reactions to your faith too.

You tell someone you'll pray for them, and they answer with some kind of New Age gibberish: "Every good vibe helps."

You tell how God gave you victory over a tough situation, and they retort, "Give yourself credit."

You express your need for God's help, and they offer that line popularized by Benjamin Franklin: "God helps those who help themselves."

You do something kind, and they step backward. "Why are you doing this? What's in it for you?" Or a sarcastic, "Well, isn't that nice."

They don't get it. To some, the story of God's goodness is a foreign language. You can't speak fluently about Jesus when your listener has only a first-grade vocabulary.

Questions invite us to move forward, giving us a clue of what the other person is ready to hear.

That McDonald's clerk wasn't the first to miss the point. More than one person responded to Better Than Ever with, "Ain't medical technology grand?" *No, no, you don't understand. There's so much more to the story.* I inhaled, ready to launch into God's part in my life story, then exhaled as quickly, for they had already turned away. And every time I felt deflated.

I shouldn't.

Questions invite us to move forward, giving us a clue of what the other person is ready to hear. At least the McDonald's clerk asked a question. And that was my cue, according to Jesus's approach to sharing the good news. He did that superbly with Nicodemus during a late-night visit (John 3). He responded to each statement and question from Nicodemus, giving enough information to draw him forward in his pursuit of the truth.

Peter and Paul followed the same strategy. They tailored their answers based on what their audience knew. Peter's crowd in Acts 2 had seen Jesus die. They were Jews well taught in the ways of God and knew one day the Messiah would come. After Peter convicted them of who Jesus was as proven by his resurrection, and of their partial responsibility in bringing about his death, they asked, "What shall we do?" (Acts 2:37). Peter gave them a detailed action plan (vv. 38–41). But the Philippian jailer in Acts 16 had never heard about Jesus. After Paul and his missionary partner Silas were miraculously set free from prison, the jailer feared for his life. In asking, "Sirs, what must I do to be saved?" he showed he was interested in saving his skin (v. 30). Paul took him to the next level and made it brief: "Believe in the Lord Jesus" (v. 31). That answer piqued the jailer's curiosity enough that he took Paul the prisoner to his home, washed him up, and listened to the rest of his story.

Like Jesus detailed in the parable of the sower (Matt. 13), some will get it, some will not, all to a varying degree. Your responsibility—and mine—is to go with what we have and keep drawing our audience further into our story. If we have a one-chance meeting, we can't go away discouraged that we didn't bring the person to the point of salvation. God is in charge, not us. He will bring someone else along to share the next gospel nugget when your McDonald's clerk is ready.

Success in proclaiming the good news is not found in how others respond. Your success is in the fact that you say anything at all and that you allow God to use you to broadcast what he has done. So keep that look of joy on your face, retain that gleam in your eye, pray for the person who didn't quite get it, and find someone else to tell.

Father God, you oversee the salvation process. Teach me how to tailor my message so those who hear will long to hear more. Show me when I've said enough for the moment, and bring along other believers who will add the next chapter to the story of your grace.

SEEING WITH FRESH EYES

Don't feel discouraged if you think you aren't sharing your faith enough. God can use snippets and one-line mentions of your relationship with him as much as the full-blown account. Be alert to those times you can tuck a piece of the message into a listener's heart, then pray that the Spirit will use what you've said.

40

Smiles

The Lord bless you and keep you; the Lord make his face shine on you and be gracious to you; the Lord turn his face toward you and give you peace.
—NUMBERS 6:24–26

In the early days of Better Than Ever, I constructed a bucket list of what I wanted to see with my new eyesight, and I intentionally set out to find those things. Along my journey, God threw in extra bonuses. I had not planned on many of those things; in fact, I didn't know how much I'd missed throughout my life until I discovered them for the first time.

Like smiles.

The first sight of my husband's smile felt like a ray of sunshine bursting through a storm-clouded sky. I'd always wondered why he didn't respond when I cracked a joke or laugh at something funny on the television. I became anxious about our relationship when he didn't speak whenever I came into the room or when I fixed a special meal. We both didn't realize I was missing his unspoken affirmation in the form of his smile. Until Better Than Ever.

I didn't see my first grandchild for five months. Now that I had experienced the power of a smile, I often asked my daughter during those months, "Has he smiled?"

"No, not yet," Katherine would say. She wanted to see that smile more than I did.

Why are smiles so important?

Smiles communicate unspoken words. In one lift of the mouth, they acknowledge our presence and the person's delight that we are there. A smile says the person hears us, agrees with what we've said, or shares our emotion of happiness or humor. It conveys that all is right with them and they are living in a season of joy and contentment. It's so cool to watch people smile back at me when I smile at them. We can know what the other is thinking without saying a thing.

We long for God's smile too. God gave Moses the words of an ancient blessing to teach to Aaron, the first high priest, and his sons, a blessing that was handed down through the generations and that we still hear and repeat today. The words tell us that God's smile is available to us (Num. 6:24–26). The phrase "make his face shine on you" feels like a smile, for a smile brightens a face, illuminating the path of communication between me and thee.

I love Jack's smile. Doing something that causes his face to break out in a grin could become addictive. That smile means he is listening to me, approving of me, and finding pleasure in me. We are one in our enjoyment of the moment, and all is well.

I want to make God smile. When I seek his face, angling to get close to him, will he turn toward me with his face aglow, overjoyed that I am there?

God not only smiles at us; he breaks out into a song of delight over us.

If I am his child and I'm seeking to follow him and claim his worldview, I've already succeeded in making God smile. He loves us with a lavish love (1 John 3:1). God not only smiles at us; he breaks out into a song of delight over us (Zeph. 3:17).

Legalism or rote, duty-bound obedience doesn't do it. God's smile broadens when we become comfortable in his presence, find joy in his service, and sit down for a visit with no intention of leaving anytime soon. He smiles when I extend my small gift of dandelion flowers, play music with rumpled rhythms for his ears alone, and share my new discoveries of the sunsets he created special for me. His face shines when I ask for his help, because helping means we get to spend time together. What grandmother could resist the tug of her cheek muscles when her wee one snuggles close and says, "I love you"? Doesn't our God react the same way?

Jack responds with a smile when I say, "You look good," or "You did well." Let's try that with God. Let's tell him, "You did such a great job with sunsets," or "I'm so glad you are a righteous and just God." I imagine his smile stretches wide when we praise him in front of others or tell them how good he is, for God delights to hear our praise. The Bible says God gets pleasure when we give sacrificially in his name (Phil. 4:18).

Making someone smile is fun. Think about the joy you can get when you work to bring a smile to God's face. Warning: it might become addictive.

Father, thank you for your delight in me. I want to tell you right now: I love you and you are the most important one in the world to me.

SEEING WITH FRESH EYES

The next time you do a good deed for another, make a right but difficult choice, or spend a moment praising God for his creation, imagine God with a huge grin on his face. You just made God smile!

41

The Food Server

But God demonstrates his own love for us in this:
While we were still sinners, Christ died for us.
—ROMANS 5:8

A server at a national chain restaurant approached our table, order pad in hand. She was overly friendly for my taste, a tattoo ran down the span of her arm, her shirttail hung out on one side, and if I'd had a dollar for every time she said the word *absolutely*, enough money would've accumulated to pay for my meal.

And I judged.

My critical spirit turned into amused annoyance. She was otherwise an okay girl. Dark-rimmed glasses, ponytail-held hair, and trim figure. And at some point, she did tuck in her drooping shirttail.

By this time, God's remaking of my reactions to other people was making me more observant. Before Better Than Ever, I boasted that I didn't see things like tattoos, shirttails, and ragged fingernails; therefore, I was immune to judgments about outward appearances. The truth is, in those days, I would not have bothered to think about the person standing before me at all. My focus would have been on getting good service for me. But as God improved the clarity of my eyes and heart to see more than I used to, the desire to see as he sees pushed aside the judgment and looked for the less obvious.

Lord, what do you want me to see about my server?

Chastened by a Spirit prick, I watched my server as she bustled from customer to customer, trying to juggle multiple orders. She forgot ketchup for Jack's steak, not because her parents failed to teach her about work ethic but because she was juggling a thousand and one details of serving a revolving door of customers. When she apologized for serving our entrée too quickly after the salad, I decided then and there how wrong I had been in how I saw this hardworking girl. From that moment on, I was going to treat her with God's grace.

A simple definition for *grace* is God's unmerited favor. In other words, grace gives what the recipient doesn't deserve. It looks beyond the faults and what I think of as flaws and foibles and instead sees what they need. Kindness. Compassion. Acceptance.

David made that choice with Mephibosheth, the grandson of King Saul, his archrival (2 Sam. 9). The boy's crippled feet made him a social outcast. His genealogy would have been enough to give David a nighttime of bad memories, as Saul had repeatedly tried to kill David and keep him from succeeding Saul as king. Yet David chose to look at who the young man was and what he needed rather than to replay repulsive memories from the past. Grandfather Saul's choices were not Mephibosheth's fault, neither was his nurse's carelessness in dropping him as she fled after Saul was killed (4:4). David invited the crippled young man to sit at the royal table.

And I could invite my harried server to sit at mine.

"You're fine," I told her. "We're not that picky about when the entrée arrives. We know you're busy and we want what's best for you."

I saw her shoulders relax. I heard her use the word *absolutely* less. And I, in turn, focused on her smile and forgot about her appearance. For a fleeting moment, I saw what Jesus saw—a person like me, both of us in need of God's grace.

Those of us who have put our faith in Jesus have discovered that he loves us through and despite the choices we've made. Long before we flaunted signs of our weakened nature, he gave the best he had—his very life. He saw not what we had done but what we needed.

> God calls us to close the gap between ourselves and others to see what he sees, a person like us in need of love, acceptance, and mercy.

He asks us to do the same. He wants us to look at the person, not the choices, to see the human heart instead of what we label as the outward fault. We won't convince people of available grace if we stand beyond their six-foot bubble with pointed fingers. God calls us to close the gap between ourselves and others to see what he sees, a person like us in need of love, acceptance, and mercy.

Jesus once asked his disciples to distribute the bread he broke from a little boy's lunch at the miraculous feeding of five thousand families (John 6:1–14). Likewise, he gives each of us a portion of his grace and asks us to distribute it to those around us. You can do that best when you offer kindness instead of criticism, a smile rather than a frown, and acceptance in the place of alienation.

Who does God call you to love this day?

> *Lord, as I encounter people today, help me see in them what you see. Partner with me to love them as you do and treat them with the same grace and mercy you have shown to me.*

SEEING WITH FRESH EYES

The next time you find yourself assessing a person's appearance, speech, or behavior, stop and listen to yourself. Are they offending your standards, or are they offending God's standards? Even if they are God's standards, how would he choose to respond to the person? Ask for his help to do as he would do in your situation.

PART 5

THE GOOD, THE UGLY, AND THE ORDINARY

42

Noseprints

Satisfy us in the morning with your unfailing love,
that we may sing for joy and be glad all our days.
—PSALM 90:14

An onslaught of several troubled days in a row left me feeling pre-occupied and distracted. Frazzled. Heartsick. My mental day planner had one overarching goal: plow through. It was then that I saw noseprints on my window. *Baxter!*

Deficit Doggie liked to perch on the back of the sofa, maneuver his snout between the curtains, watch squirrels and autumn leaves zoom past his domain, and furiously wiggle his Pembroke corgi tail stump. He loved keeping watch when I retrieved the mail. His perky face glared at me as I returned to the house each morning, and I would tap the window just to antagonize him. It became our special game.

Why had I never noticed his nose-to-glass contact before? Ah, it was this thing called a surgery that gave me Better Than Ever eyesight. No need to put my nose against the window. I could see the prints while standing five feet across the room.

I know it was five feet. I measured.

Great. I can see my dirty window. Why today of all days?

It was the Wednesday after Thanksgiving. Both adult daughters had come home for the weekend, and the three of us spent time doing what we never normally do—shopping on Black Friday and drinking coffee together. We were refreshed, ready to return to the groove of our routines. After the girls left, life lurched into the complicated. There ought to be a rule. Nothing bad should happen the week after a holiday. Let's ease back into this life thing so we can savor the sweeter moments.

It was not to be. Monday morning, an assailant plowed his car into a crowd of university students two blocks from Christine's former college residence hall. I knew those streets and spent the day blinking back tears as I wondered if family friends and campus ministry workers were hurt in the attack. That evening, moments before our women's fellowship group began our meeting, a dear saint of God felt her arm snap as she got out of her car. Bev rushed her to the hospital with Jack following in his car close behind, and our group of women delayed our program so we could pray. The next morning, our family made difficult decisions regarding my mother-in-law's care. The day ended with Jack coming home from an after-school children's program, weary and discouraged from an extra chaotic event that had not taken into account the pent-up energy of children the week after Thanksgiving.

"No more bad stuff," I posted on Facebook. "I declare today 'Wonderful Wednesday.'" I could use a little good news and I wasn't willing to wait another day.

Then I saw the smudge of noseprints caught in the glint of sunlight. I peered over my heartache and smiled. My silly dog.

The week wasn't so bad, really. Other smile moments had happened. Making hot chocolate mix with an older friend. Talking long-distance with my mother. An awesome Bible study session. My blog article about the campus attack bringing comfort to my campus ministry friends.

And doggie noseprints.

God mixes in the good to soften the blows of the bad and invites us to look harder for joy. David acknowledged that truth when he asked God, "Make us glad for as many days as you have afflicted us, for as many years as we have seen trouble. May your deeds be shown to your servants, your splendor to their children" (Ps. 90:15–16).

Heartaches happen, days have trouble, but God's unfailing love smooths the rough edges and makes us stronger. The Lord could have allowed me to see that noseprint on any sunny day, but he chose a time when my soul was weary and needed the strength found in a smile.

The shadow of your troubles might camouflage your stash of joy, but the joy is still there, for it runs like a golden strand through the trials. You and I have a choice. We can focus our attention on the relentless onslaught of hard moments, or we can turn away, allowing them to slip to the periphery of our spirits so God's special gifts can instead fill our central vision, where we can see the best. When we step back and allow our troubles to be part of the bigger picture of God's plan, two things happen. First, the bad stuff loses its menacing look. And second, we notice the tucked-in details of the joyful moments.

What did God do with those smudges that marked that week after Thanksgiving? The campus attack gave Christian students opportunities to show care for others. Our fellowship group surrounded our beloved sister with love and prayer and found ourselves strengthened by the tenacity of her faith even though she'd been a Christ follower for only two years. Other smudges called me to renewed dependence on God's promises that he would reign supreme, make redemptive use of the bad situations, and work all things together for my good and his glory (Rom. 8:28).

Let the little things of the ordinary moment remind you that all is not bad, God still loves you, and you will get through this tough time.

Let the little things of the ordinary moment remind you that all is not bad, God still loves you, and you will get through this tough time.

For all of life's moments can be softened or made more brittle by our perspective. Each smudge bears a bit of the beautiful, for God reigns within each moment.

Hold on. The sun is coming to shine through the smudge.

Lord, whenever life events hit me hard, remind
me of the smile moments. Help me find touches of
joy tucked within the hard days so I can yet again
praise you.

SEEING WITH FRESH EYES

Are you having a bad day? Take a closer look. What happy moments has God tucked into your troubled day? Thank him for each one.

43

Emergency Signs

Whether you turn to the right or to the left, your
ears will hear a voice behind you, saying, "This is
the way; walk in it."
—ISAIAH 30:21

I love to fly. I've often said I wasn't afraid to fly by myself. Yet strands of undefined tension wrapped around my confidence whenever I listened to a flight attendant's safety instructions. My concern was not whether the plane would crash; statistics show that airplanes are safer than cars. Fear came from wondering how I would cope in an emergency situation. I'd have to figure out how to exit on my own and follow the crowd, or slow everyone down with my pleas for help from people intent on getting themselves out of the aircraft. Worse yet, what if I was a detriment to someone else's survival in my inability to help them?

Fear is the story of what-ifs. Whenever fear whispered a litany of what could happen, I shrugged it away, determined God and I would figure it out somehow.

Then I saw emergency signs.

Our family flew to Atlanta for my mother-in-law's funeral. I buckled my seat belt and caught a glimpse of a red glow. I nudged Jack, softening my serious discovery with a silly grin. "When did airplanes install exit signs?"

"They've always been there." Consternation spread over Jack's face as he realized the truth. "You've never been able to see them before?" His expression spoke volumes: *And I let you travel by yourself?*

The flight attendant started her spiel. I followed her pointed fingers and looked downward. The bait was irresistible. "There are lights along the floorboards too. So that's how people know how to get out if there's an emergency landing."

What a relief. At least now I knew which direction to head. I wasn't so helpless anymore. Or was I? My sober moment returned. Were the lights enough?

Signs, lights, and spouses have their limits. Any of those might fail to provide the help and guidance we need to get out of harm's way. Maybe that's the lesson God tried to teach the army captain Gideon, when he replaced ground troops with trumpets and torches (Judg. 7).

The Israelites had been under the oppression of the powerful Midianites for seven long years. God had promised to save the Israelites by Gideon's leadership, so Gideon gathered as many men as he could from the people of Israel.

"You have too many men," God told Gideon. "Send those who tremble with fear home."

Gideon sent the fraidy-cats home.

"You still have too many," God said. "Send home those who drink from cupped hands."

Gideon sent home the men who drank from the nearby spring with cupped hands and only kept the men who lapped the water like dogs, a mere three hundred of them. To these men, Gideon distributed bowls, trumpets, and torches. And with these men and those tools, Gideon overcame the vast Midianite army.

God trimmed Gideon's resources to show him his need to rely not on his own ability but on God alone. At any time, what we have might not be enough to bail us out of trouble. Even those with strong bodies and perfect eyesight might not be able to stop the inevitable.

The only one we can fully trust is God himself.

As our flight to Atlanta lifted off, I asked myself, *Has God not taken care of me before?*

Pictures from the past pushed aside remaining fear.

The flight in a vintage World War II turboprop that took off from Pittsburgh, crossed over a sixty-degree-dropping cold front, and landed safely in Canton, Ohio, despite boulder-sized turbulence.

That time when eighteen-month-old Christine reached a hand to the kitchen counter, yanked the coffee carafe from its stand, and threw it over her shoulder onto my kitchen floor strewn with dirty laundry. I couldn't see the broken glass, so I called a neighbor to help. "I don't understand," she said as she shook out piles of clothes and took the broom from my hand. "Glass should be all over these clothes, but it landed in only one small pile on the bare floor." I understood. Had I not prayed every night that God would protect my babies in ways I could not?

Nothing will happen to you without God's foreknowledge.

Twenty years later, Katherine was heading home for Christmas when she heard a loud knocking sound from her right front tire. Taking the last interstate exit on the west side of Dayton, Ohio, before heading into miles of snow-strewn farmland, she found a tire store at the bottom of the ramp. After the repairman put the car on the rack, she approached to look at the damaged tire, but he waved her back, cautioning, "Don't touch. It could blow." He was astounded that the tire had not exploded on the highway.

And then there was the day when a straight-line windstorm ripped through central North Carolina. Jack entered our newly purchased house with an armload of possessions and turned to shut the door, only to see a tree limb fly like a missile past where he had stood seconds before.

Nothing will happen to you without God's foreknowledge. He will protect you, sometimes in ways that can be credited only to him. If you're injured, he'll walk you through that difficult season. And if he deems it time for your life on this earth to end, why, heaven awaits if you've put your trust in him.

Emergency signs point the way to safety—that's their job. They give the information we need to sidestep danger. I'm grateful for flight attendants who have the training to keep us safe. I'm thankful for a husband who is strong, sighted, and sensitive to my needs. Ultimately, however, any earthly resources are no guarantee of safety or deliverance.

God, on the other hand, has promised to never leave or forsake us. He is the one who will strengthen, supply, and embolden us with peace and confidence so we don't have to give in to panic.

What makes you panic? Perhaps *panic* is too strong of a word. But each of us has something in our lives that causes us to shift our feet in discomfort, knowing that we are not quite as in control as we'd like to be. The next time you are in a situation where you think you've done all you can do and gathered all that you need but you still have that nagging sense that it's not enough, breathe. God is ultimately in charge, he loves you deeply and dearly, and he has the ability to protect you in ways you may never see. In the meantime, he is not leaving you.

The sign of his presence is the best assurance of all.

I will be with you.

No fear.

> *Father, thank you for all that you provide in this*
> *world to keep me safe. Ultimately, my trust is in*
> *you. You are the one who will never fail me or*
> *abandon me.*

SEEING WITH FRESH EYES

Choosing to trust God for his protection is a mindset, an intentional decision made before danger happens. Tell God you do trust him to care for you and those you love in whatever crisis you might face next.

44

More Snow

But I tell you, love your enemies and pray for those
who persecute you, that you may be children of
your Father in heaven. He causes his sun to rise
on the evil and the good, and sends rain on the
righteous and the unrighteous.
—MATTHEW 5:44–45

The first winter after Better Than Ever, snow fascinated me. How much snow could I see? How thick must the snowfall be before I could see it midair? How far out could I see snow falling?

That last question is what interested me the most. Before Better Than Ever, I was lucky to see a single snowflake fall past my nose. Now I could see both those close-up snowflakes and swirling snow farther out, giving the snow a three-dimensional look. Not sure how else to describe what I was seeing, I dubbed it "snow behind snow."

I kept challenging my left eye to stretch beyond its six-foot perimeter. *Let's see what's out there.* Before, the radar map on my phone and the snow piling on my driveway told me snow was falling over a broader area than my eyes could see. Now I could see it for myself. Snow really was falling on other places and, yes, on other people, as well as on me.

That may sound simplistic, or as we said when my girls were teenagers, "Well, duh." But living constantly within a six-foot bubble lures us to become me-focused. A shortsighted view seeps into the rest of life, and I found it easy to not think about anything happening beyond my little world. Out of sight, out of mind, right? Every human being struggles with self-absorption, yet I speculate it is a bigger temptation for anyone with a physical disability, chronic illness, or constant pain. My own physical limits shout my needs loud enough to muffle the concerns of others.

Yet Jesus calls us to put others first, to think of them more highly than ourselves. He never lets those with physical limits, illness, or pain off the hook. Jesus told his disciples, "The Son of Man did not come to be served, but to serve, and to give his life as a ransom for many" (Matt. 20:28). Jesus modeled that others-oriented focus despite our own extenuating circumstances when he arranged for the care of Mary, his mother, while he hung on the cross (John 19:26–27). Even in his greatest agony, he thought about his mother's need for protection and provision.

I wish I could be like Jesus. As difficult as Satan's temptations and the crucifixion must have been for him, he was perfect and sinless. He forever had his mind on the bigger picture of God's plan. Me? I've got a lifetime of me-moments dogging my heels. It's not so easy for this sin-disabled brain and body. My old nature constantly cries out, *Don't I have to take care of me?*

The snow behind snow gave me a visual reminder of the need to move past my own myopathy. I traced the path of the snow falling ten feet from me. As far as I could see, snow was blanketing the ground in an equal layer, playing no favorites.

Snow falls within everyone's six-foot bubble. The same amount of snow that falls at my feet falls at the feet of others. It doesn't matter to snow whether I've been a good girl that day or robbed a bank. Nor does it care if I live alone or have three rambunctious children capering through the snow. The items on my to-do list or the burdens my neighbor carries aren't its concern either. As Jesus taught, rain falls on the just and the unjust. The sun blesses the righteous and the corrupt (Matt. 5:45).

> If God . . . makes no distinction between me and the next person, and I want to take on the image of Christ, shouldn't I do the same?

If God, through the falling snow, makes no distinction between me and the next person, and I want to take on the image of Christ, shouldn't I do the same? Shouldn't I care about how snow affects my neighbor as much as I do about its impact on me?

Empathy is the ability to see life from the viewpoint of another. That means having a willingness to walk life in the shoes of someone else, and no one did that better than Jesus. He took off his heavenly slippers in exchange for Jewish sandals and walked dusty, rock-strewn roads instead of streets of gold.

Love and mercy look at life from within someone else's six-foot bubble. Once you and I put ourselves inside the brain and living situation of another person, we'll better understand what that person needs and the whys behind their choices or reactions. I wonder if that was part of the reason Jesus told his disciples to walk an extra mile for those who forced them to walk one mile (Matt. 5:41).

The Romans occupied the land of Israel during the time Jesus walked this earth. At any time, a Roman soldier could pluck someone out of their daily schedule and conscript them to carry their gear for a mile. That and numerous other atrocities made many Jews seethe with indignation.

Jesus called his disciples not only to let go of such resentment but to willingly walk two miles instead of one. And he calls us to walk out of our daily plans to do the same. In that extra-mile moment, you and I have the chance to see the life and soul of those who would take advantage of us for their own selfish reasons. What better time to see that unreasonable person as a person, not as an intruder like the Jewish people regarded the Romans to be?

Who frustrates you? Try this. Mentally insert yourself into five moments of that person's life. Would you handle their life any differently? Would you be frazzled and forgetful if you were a mother to two severely handicapped children or the spouse of someone caught in an addiction? Would you be socially clumsy if you were alone for weeks at a time, then finally able to come to a social gathering? Would you be more inclined to be a people pleaser if you worked in an environment where you were constantly barraged and beaten down for whatever you did?

Once you know their inside story, you will be better equipped to be a blessing of mercy. By sharing some of the burden they carry, you can meet their needs more effectively because now you know what your friend faces and how circumstances must seem from their vantage point.

Who needs you to step into their snow pile? In what ways can you look past the poor choices or less than ideal circumstances? Is there a small task, gift, or word of encouragement you can give to help them see Jesus's love and care for them?

It might be something as simple as shoveling the snow from their sidewalk.

Lord, who needs to see your mercy today? I want to step inside lives, see needs, and catch a vision of how you can use me to meet those needs. Help me.

SEEING WITH FRESH EYES

Go somewhere where you can people watch. Select one person and imagine what it would be like to live their life from what you observe about them. How would Jesus show mercy to them?

45

Wall Smudges

For God, who said, "Let light shine out of darkness," made his light shine in our hearts to give us the light of the knowledge of God's glory displayed in the face of Christ.
—2 CORINTHIANS 4:6

*M*y hand poised over the bathroom light switch. There it lay, unmoving, above the switch panel, marring my beautiful peach-colored bathroom wall paint—a black smudge. Awareness turned to alarm. I grabbed a sponge. With a few furious scrubs, the black disappeared.

First, doggie noseprints; now black marks. How distressing. People have to put up with seeing that stuff? I hadn't expected better vision to allow me to see what I'd rather not see.

When you look straight at something, you are using your central vision. When you see something out of the corner of your eye, you are using your peripheral vision. Glaucoma can reduce your side vision, and maladies like macular degeneration can rob you of central vision. I have an idea. Let's have something called selective vision. The only things you can see clearly are the good and beautiful. All ugly, bad, or yucky stuff blurs into the background.

Yes, I know. Lovely idea. Not realistic.

Unable to see the dinge and smudges of surfaces, I used to label friends who talked about cleaning their walls as fussy housekeepers. If walls needed cleaning, what else in my house belonged in the unacceptable category? What did visitors think about the dog hair, cobwebs, and dust on end tables that I couldn't see? Did they think I was a bad housekeeper or talk behind their hands in pity? I know they talked. I sometimes heard them. "Karen doesn't see it. Perhaps she should hire a housekeeper. Why doesn't her family help her? Doesn't she know?"

No, I didn't know. Before Better Than Ever, blindness was bliss. Out of sight, out of mind. If you don't mind, it doesn't matter.

Now it mattered because I could see the mess. I was not happy. Wall smudges were not on my bucket list of what I wanted to use my newfound vision to see.

If we want to see life from God's perspective, we have to be willing to see what he sees . . . even the grime of our imperfections.

Unfortunately, wall smudges don't just exist on my physical walls. I've discovered them on my spiritual walls too. When God sheds his light into our darkened lives, we'll see smudges we never knew existed. Spiritual blindness leaves us clueless because we don't know that life could be any different. The closer we move toward God, the more the light of his holiness shines on our lives. The more his light shines, the more mess we'll see: cracks, fault lines, and blemishes. An overall grime we didn't want anyone else to notice. Distress turns to panic: Have others observed I'm not as cleaned up as I pretend to be?

I don't like knowing I've blown it, do you? I wish I could become selective in this faith walk. I'd rather bask in God's loving care and spend moments in wonder at the beauty of his creation. I don't want to see the areas of my life that need more than a sponge swipe. Pride sells an excellent set of blinders, don't you think?

Yes, all of us have blind spots that keep us oblivious to our personal foibles and unrighteous attitudes. But if we want to see life from God's perspective, we have to be willing to see what he sees in the same way he sees it, even the grime of our imperfections.

What about grace? Doesn't God's forgiveness tune out our sin?

Absolutely. But I had to see that black spot before I could do something about it. Likewise, the spiritual seeker needs to know how damaging their separation from God is before accepting God's perfect solution of grace. The journey toward intimacy with God means giving God permission to open our eyes so we can see the areas not yet surrendered to him and then allowing him to work with us to clean up those messes.

Here's the bonus blessing: We'll see the difference when the smudges are gone. Once I cleaned my house, targeting the newly sighted dirty spots, the peach paint in my bathroom brightened into a rosy glow, faucet fixtures shined, and the wood grain of end tables glimmered with a deeper beauty. Before in my darkened world, I didn't know if I had cleaned well enough. Now, housecleaning became fun because I could see the results and a clean house is such a pretty sight.

I still don't like the dirty spots my bad choices leave. But I've discovered that when I am patient instead of intolerant, when I speak graciously instead of with irritable criticism, and when I pray about a situation rather than fretting, my life shines brightly enough for me and those around me to notice and appreciate. The difference is incredible.

I'd much rather live by God's clear-cut righteousness than by my blurred way of thinking. I still mess up frequently. But when I remember how I've changed and how I'm growing, the knowledge of that progress gives me more contentment than a clean wall.

What smudges your relationship with Jesus? Is it hard to look at the stains of consequences past mistakes have made? Focus on those mistakes long enough to decide how you and God want you to be different. Then set your sights on how God can help you change and how beautiful you will look in the remaking.

Lord, give me the courage to see myself as you see me and the humility to ask for your help to clean up my life and make me more like you.

SEEING WITH FRESH EYES

Dare to look inside your heart. What keeps you from being your best for Jesus? Certain books, apps, or relationships? Attitudes, grudges, or memories of the past? If you have trouble thinking of one, pray that God will reveal one of your smudges. Tell him that, with his help, you are willing to let it go.

46

Bugs

*Finally, brothers and sisters, whatever is true,
whatever is noble, whatever is right, whatever is
pure, whatever is lovely, whatever is admirable—
if anything is excellent or praiseworthy—
think about such things.*
—PHILIPPIANS 4:8

Out of sight, out of mind. The saying was my survival code. If you don't know it's there, it doesn't bug you. Oblivion can be rather nice. That's how I felt about flies and frogs, gnats and bats.

Then Better Than Ever happened. I discovered yet again what else I'd missed when I felt a fly tickle my hand while I was reading. A fly with green iridescent wings. I thought all flies were black. It was kind of pretty.

Before, I sometimes could see flies on my skin, but not in detail and never in midair. Now I discovered that the sky was not blank air. So that's why people commented about birds, spiders, and dust particles. Those black spots I'd seen weren't floaters after all. Transfixed by the sight of airborne matter one morning, I stood at my kitchen window, attempting to identify what I saw.

My husband stood beside me. "The sky is filled with stuff," I sputtered. "And you see better than I do. How do you put up with all the detail?"

He shrugged and headed toward his recliner. "I tune it out."

Several days later, he fiddled with his hearing aid. "That lawn mower is so loud. Don't you find that annoying?"

Orneriness ruled. "I tune it out." *Gotcha.*

Clutter fills my life. How do I manage all the fluffy stuff? I have choices: I can remove the clutter. I can let it distract me from what I'm doing. Or I can tune it out.

Some clutter is within my control. I can clear my desk, wash the dishes, and not fill my mind with unimportant news details or computer games. Other clutter, like a husband's sock-strewn floor, a neighbor's constant chatter, or a child's annoying tic, mocks me in my inability to control my world. Yet, within the uncontrolled, I choose how I respond. I can make a big deal about the problem and how I feel about it. Or I can tune it out.

Jesus would have you and me concentrate on what matters most to him.

I can spend hours of my day stewing over my spouse's faults or the oh-so-human aspects of humans who intersect my daily life. Or I can think about Jesus and his perfection and look for the way he has made each person beautiful. You and I can have hissy fits about fake news or corrupt politicians. Or we can set those reports to the side so we can focus on how God has called us to live.

Jesus would have you and me concentrate on what matters most to him.

He already set the example. He refused to allow sin to get in the way of our relationship with him. Instead, he dealt with the problem of sin on the cross and then chose to no longer dwell on it, to not hold our sin against us. Micah 7:19 promises, "You will again have compassion on us; you will tread our sins underfoot and hurl all our iniquities into the depths of the sea." Once you and I accept his gift of grace by putting our trust in him, God chooses to no longer look at our sin. When we cry out for God's forgiveness and accept his terms for payment, he takes our sins, buries them in the depths, and then turns his back, refusing to look at them again. He tunes them out.

That's forgiveness. That's what God does for me. That's what he asks me to do for the person next in line. He invites you to do that as well.

When someone irritates, annoys, or even commits a crime against us, we have a choice. Do we become bugs ourselves and participate in a self-righteous criticism of their sin sickness? Do we fixate on how awful the world is and how ugly people can be?

Jesus gives us an alternate response to our buggy kind of world. "Set your minds on things above, not on earthly things" (Col. 3:2). Our old life of sin is dead and gone, buried in the deepest sea, so he asks us to fix our eyes on things of eternal importance, looking ahead, beyond, and above, where he is. Jesus is part of eternity, and eternity is where we're headed (vv. 3–4). Forgiveness looks past the sin to what the sinner can become.

How do you look past the faults and quirks of others when they move into your line of vision? How do you restrain yourself from putting a magnifying lens on those things that frustrate you or cause a rush of resentment and anger within you?

Oh, my friend, I invite you to forgive as Jesus forgave you. Turn your back on those things that bug you, the sins and poor choices of those who have caused hurt. Move those flaws and foibles into your blurry peripheral vision and tune them out.

Instead, look fully at Jesus in all his loveliness. Study his creation and eagerly look toward eternity, where his justice, love, and glory will reign forever. Focus on what is true, just, lovely, and praiseworthy. For when we stand in the light of God's glory, we'll see life issues from God's perspective and as part of his plan instead of as distractions and annoyances. We'll put the placeholder of his presence in everything we do and in everything we encounter.

Even flies with iridescent wings.

Lord, this moment I fix my eyes on you. As I'm tempted by annoying distractions, I give you permission to remind me of your presence so I can turn my gaze back to you.

SEEING WITH FRESH EYES

Determine to do some "pest control." Name someone who bugs you. Ask God to help you demonstrate his love, patience, and encouragement to that person today.

47

Squirrels

Do not conform to the pattern of this world, but be
transformed by the renewing of your mind. Then
you will be able to test and approve what God's
will is—his good, pleasing and perfect will.
—ROMANS 12:2

*D*espite my efforts to tune out birds, gnats, and other moving mid-air objects, I kept getting sidetracked—by squirrels, of all things. Power walks now included multiple pause points to watch them play hide-and-seek with me as I peered around tree trunks to catch their antics.

I had told my husband I was going for just a short walk. But he is a perceptive man. He knew Better Than Ever was distracting enough to stretch short into long and give me stories to tell upon my return home.

"I saw a squirrel. Six feet up. He jumped from one trunk to another." I protected Jack from further blather about the finer details: how the squirrel clung upside down to the trunk, hoping to blend in unseen, but his bushy golden tail flopped on top of him, disclosing his presence. Silly squirrel. I had smothered a laugh and inched closer, hoping to see more. He skittered sideways, throwing his tail to the opposite side, and his body camouflaged into the mottled brown wood. Then he disappeared among the branches. Our hide-and-seek game was over, and the squirrel had won.

I looked at the clock, then at my waiting to-do list. While watching the squirrel might not be bad necessarily, what would happen if I neglected all the other things and chased after the proverbial squirrels for hours or days or months?

Tell me, please. How am I supposed to know what to tune out and what is worth more than a cursory glance?

Ah, one of the big questions of life.

Life management is made up of a myriad of decisions, far more complicated than whether I should spend my time looking at squirrels or bugs, what I should fix for supper, or which color socks to wear. Life coaches make a living by helping people choose how they spend their time, money, and energy. It's all about prioritizing and balance, they tell us.

The decisions become even more complicated when you follow Jesus.

As God transforms your life and you see beyond the seen, you become acquainted with another way to live. You learn the difference between right and wrong, good and evil, just and unjust, and that knowledge presents more choices than you had before you decided to follow Jesus. Some things in life may be good but not best—or not best at this time. Motivation becomes part of the mix, for the first chapter of Jesus's famous Sermon on the Mount emphasizes that the attitude with which we approach our choices is as important as the action (Matt. 5).

Help. Ten simple rules would make this Christian life so much easier.

Paul makes this distinction to the Corinthians: "'I have the right to do anything,' you say—but not everything is beneficial. 'I have the right to do anything'—but not everything is constructive. No one should seek their own good, but the good of others" (1 Cor. 10:23–24).

While our salvation is not based on our obedience to a law, God invites us to live a life founded on our love for Jesus.

And that means choices, lots of choices, often between good, better, and best.

How to spend time.

How to spend money.

Which friends to spend time with.

Where to go on vacation.

How to act while on vacation.

It gets messy.

How do you and I choose what is best? Squirrels or bugs? Ignore it all and power walk home?

I'm so relieved we have the Word of God and the person of the Holy Spirit to guide us through our life choices. Consistently making right choices takes time—in fact, a lifetime. But God is gracious, ever patient, and a fantastic teacher. And in time, the decisions become easier and more intuitive.

> The secret to making better and best choices with confidence is to become so familiar with God's ways that you begin to think like him.

The secret to making better and best choices with confidence is to become so familiar with God's ways that you begin to think like him. You don't have to wonder what he wants. The words he wrote in Scripture reveal his heart and passion. As God shows you how to look at life from his vantage point, you will *want* to do what pleases him and what is good for others.

Where do you start? First, make the commitment to no longer conform to the world's standards (Rom. 12:2). At the beginning of your day, determine to see the world through God's eyes (Eph. 1:18). The Bible serves as a training manual that outlines godly living (2 Tim. 3:16), so read it.

Finally, be patient with yourself. The skill of making good decisions takes practice. God's transformation process leaves room for you to make mistakes and gives you the grace to fail so ultimately you can succeed. Take a deep breath and resolve, with God's help, not to make the same mistake tomorrow.

In the meantime, go watch a squirrel . . . but perhaps not all day.

Maybe that's part of God's rationale behind squirrel creation. Pausing to watch nature at play gives us a break from keeping up with the more serious plot points of life, as good as relaxing with a cup of tea or having a chat with a friend. It resets your sights, clears the clutter, and realigns your spirit of discernment to think anew with the mind of Christ.

Lord, help me carve out time today to pause, rest, and sit at your feet so I am better equipped to see my life choices from your point of view.

SEEING WITH FRESH EYES

What distracted you today? How can you turn those disruptions into restful resets without getting off track from the important things of life? If you are unsure, ask God for wisdom. He's promised he will give it to you.

48

Carpet

Whatever you do, work at it with all your heart, as
working for the Lord, not for human masters.
—COLOSSIANS 3:23

*B*efore Better Than Ever, I wanted to prove I could do anything despite my visual loss. But years of life experience showed me I had my limits. After surgery, enthralled with my newfound vision, I was ready to try all those things I had reluctantly agreed I couldn't do. I felt liberated. The sky's the limit? Hardly. I was full throttle in "I really can do anything" mode.

One swipe with a rug cleaner blew that theory to smithereens.

The carpet was filthy. Jack's back pain had increased. "Hey, sweetie, I can do it," I offered. "I can see better now. No guesswork. See? The sweeper makes marks that tell me where to begin the next row. Go away. I've got this."

Alas, I still had limited depth perception. On the first swipe, I promptly broke the plastic corner shield as I edged too close to the wall.

Do you ever feel, like me, that you have to be able to do all things? Be good at whatever you attempt? Say yes to whatever is asked of you? Juggle all the demands without dropping a single ball?

Let's learn together. Give it up.

But we want to feel useful. The job won't get done if we don't do it. There's no one else but me. *Can't* doesn't belong in my vocabulary.

Oh, friends. Do you hear the pride in *I can*? Pride weasels its way into our lives in the form of stubbornness and rebellion, and we buy into the delusion that we'll show weakness if we dare to use the *can't* word.

What is wrong with weakness? When we are weak, God is strong. When we work together in partnership with the community of believers, we are stronger yet. "A cord of three strands is not quickly broken" (Eccl. 4:12), but that cord is made of individual strands who are not strong enough in and of themselves. Part of God's strengthening is the provision of like-hearted friends to work beside us. But in order for us to experience the full extent of God's strengthening, each of us has to admit there are some things we cannot do on our own.

Too often I tell myself, *Doesn't the Bible say we can do all things through Christ who gives us strength (Phil. 4:13)? If I just trusted Jesus more, I could do this.* God must shake his head every time I think that.

Philippians 4:13 says "can," not "must." It may not be in your or another's best interest for you to do it all. The trick is to refocus on the overall scheme of the day.

Why is it good to not do everything?

Doing it all isn't the wisest use of our time, energy, or giftedness. Choosing to channel our energy into what we do well means we may need to let go of the tasks we struggle with or think we ought to be able to do. I love Rhett Butler's response to Ashley Wilkes in the movie version of *Gone with the Wind* after Ashley is shot. Ashley, needing to move to the bedroom, insists he can do it himself. Rhett's response often rings in my mind: "You can do it, but is it worth the extra effort?"

God never intended for us to do everything on our own. He prefers choirs over leading-lady divas. Solo acts deprive others of the chance to develop their skills or play to their strengths. Teamwork promotes unity, for there is sweet satisfaction in sharing a common goal. And we'll accomplish more when we involve others. Paul conveyed that message in 1 Corinthians 12 when he reminded his readers that not everyone is a foot or an eye. We each have our distinct job that adds to the whole of the project.

We all need each other. We need what each person has to contribute.

We all need each other. We need what each person has to contribute.

Letting go becomes a lesson in humility. It requires an honest scrutiny of who you are, what you have to offer, and what is best left to others. It calls for an awareness of and respect for the gifts and underdeveloped strengths God has conferred on those around you. We are all works in progress, incomplete, and messy, with backpacks full of past mistakes, chipped pride, and hidden agendas. God's greatest work happens when we do our best at whatever we undertake (Col. 3:17), not when we tackle every job on the roster.

The time may come when God calls you to a task that you don't think you can handle or when no one else is available. In those moments, God will fill you with strength and wisdom to do the impossible. Until that time, you and I both need each other.

And me with my carpet cleaner? My childlike exuberance was admirable, but next time, I think I might take a humble pill and say, "Hey, sweetie, I may not do this well, but I'll do my best. Can we work together to get the job done?" Who knows? The moments spent together might be the best part of the job, just like Thanksgiving dinner when everyone brings a dish or works in the kitchen together to make the feast happen.

Give yourself permission to say, "I can't." Better yet, say, "This is not the best use of my energy or resources. I am more complete when I tap into the abilities of other people." Be comfortable in your own skin. Know your limits, release them to God, seek his strength, and accept who he sends to work with you.

It just might be more fun.

Lord, I can't do everything. I need you and I need
your people. Together, through you, we can do
great things for you.

SEEING WITH FRESH EYES

Make a list of your weekly household, civic, or church responsibilities. Are there any you should be giving to someone else? Choose one task where you can invite a friend, family member, or colleague to work with you. Pray that God will help you encourage each other as you work together.

49

PowerPoint Slides

*You, LORD, are my lamp; the LORD turns my
darkness into light.*
—2 SAMUEL 22:29

One of the greatest joys of my new eyesight was seeing song lyrics projected on PowerPoint slides at the front of our church's worship center.

While digital technology has done much to encourage greater worship participation, it locked me out. I love to sing, and I love to sing God's praises. I would be near tears when song leaders introduced new songs and I had no access to the words. I so wanted to be included, but I wasn't. When I heard worship team members complain that they couldn't hear people singing, I bit my lip to keep from saying, *I would if I could.*

Now, Better Than Ever allowed me to see the screen from the middle of our congregation's small auditorium. What a relief. I finally felt like I could be part of my church family as I actively joined them in song. I didn't have to look different as I stood in silence while everyone else lifted their praise to God.

My perception was wrong, though. I had always been a part of my church family. I was participating in worship even if I wasn't doing what everyone else was doing or in the same way everyone else was doing it.

An endless list of reasons can stand between us and worshipping in the ways we prefer. And it's easy to let those obstacles dictate how or whether we worship.

If I can't sing, I'm not worshipping.

If I'm not in a church building Sunday morning, I can't worship God.

If I'm not following a certain order of activities, it's just not worship.

Not true. Not true at all.

Darius, the Babylonian king, passed an edict prohibiting prayer addressed to anyone but the king. That meant no public prayer meetings. But Daniel, a high-ranking official and a godly man, continued his habit of praying and giving thanks to God three times a day as he knelt in front of an open window (Dan. 6).

Another king named Herod put the apostle Peter in prison, intending to execute him the next day. Despite legitimate concerns about persecution, a group of Christ followers still gathered for a late-night prayer meeting (Acts 12).

Jewish tradition did not allow the establishment of a local synagogue for formal Sabbath worship unless there were at least ten adult males present. That didn't stop a group of God-fearing women who chose to meet at a riverbank to pray and worship. That's where the apostle Paul found them and told them about Jesus (Acts 16:13).

Believers in restricted countries around the world find ways to meet, even when laws say they must gather in groups of less than five.

My grandfather became a believer at age eighty-six. Nearly stone-deaf, unable to hear the words of the sermon, and finding the music painful rather than inspiring—true for many hard-of-hearing folks— Grandpa still came to church until his health deteriorated in the final two months. You couldn't keep him away. Hearing issues were not going to deter my grandpa.

What restrictions can cause you to falter in your worship?

True worship of God does not depend on external props, routines, or programs. John 4 tells of a woman who questioned Jesus about worship practices. The Jews said the only place to worship God was in the temple in Jerusalem, but the woman's people group, the Samaritans, said their local mountain was good enough (John 4:19–20). If we aren't in the right place or in a sanctified building, is our worship still acceptable to God?

Worship is a response of our heart to who God is and what he has done.

Jesus's concise answer epitomizes the essence of worship. True worshippers honor God in spirit and in truth (v. 23). If that's in place, little else matters. A search through the Old Testament shows that worship is a response of our heart to who God is and what he has done.

Abraham sent his servant to his hometown to find a wife for his son Isaac. When Abraham's servant recognized God's part in leading him on the right path to find Abraham's relatives, he paused and gave praise to God in front of an animals' water trough (Gen. 24:11–27).

When the Israelites enslaved in Egypt heard Moses's report that God saw their misery and cared, they didn't wait till the next Sabbath meeting to thank their God. They immediately responded with worship (Exod. 4:31).

King David, hearing that Solomon now sat on the throne, worshipped God on his bed for allowing his son to succeed him (1 Kings 1:47).

God cares more about the why behind our worship than the how, where, or when.

The psalmist urges us, "Ascribe to the LORD the glory due his name" (Ps. 29:2). Why do we gather together to publicly praise God? Because we've seen his handiwork in creation, his power at work in our lives, and his nature as described in his Word, we love to rejoice and share good news together. Our worship showcases our level of faith in our God to a watching world.

If the why of worship is firmly in place, you can still worship God no matter what external roadblocks you face. The starting point is a heart willing to seek after God and express gratitude for what he has done. And when you reflect on how he has turned your darkness into light, nothing will stop you from gathering with other believers to honor the God you love.

So get creative.

Get stubborn.

When the Evil One lies to you, telling you that you can't worship effectively without the resources you've always enjoyed, rise up in defiance and say, "Oh yeah?"

Not "Oh well." No defeatist mentality allowed. Let's allow nothing to deter us from the worship of our God.

Soon after I discovered I could read PowerPoint slides, our church replaced the large roll-up screen with a flat-screen monitor and mounted it to the far wall. I was back to where I was before Better Than Ever, no longer able to read the lyrics. By this time, I had a better vision of how to worship God, and I decided to be proactive. I called the church office to obtain a list of songs for the upcoming worship service. I then searched the internet for the lyrics, copied them into a Word document, and printed them out in a font size I could see. Yes, I looked different from everyone else as I juggled my multiple sheets of paper, but, hey, I already looked different when I stood like a statue, unsinging. At least now I could sing.

The best part is that the office staff caught my dilemma. Now they print out song sheets for me and the two other visually impaired church members. See what can happen when you go on the worship offensive?

Paul reminded his readers that nothing in heaven or earth can get in God's way of loving us (Rom. 8:38–39). Can you and I have that same attitude toward worship, a determination that nothing will keep us from praising our God? He has done so much for us—he deserves our unhindered praise, that whatever-it-takes tenacity.

If you can't sing, pray.

If you can't go somewhere, worship where you are.

If your government restricts worship to no more than five people, find five people. If fifteen people want to worship, hold three services.

Your efforts just might make it possible for others to worship him too.

> *Lord, I want to worship you. Give me ideas of how I can worship you without the externals I'm used to so I can praise and honor you anytime, anywhere.*

SEEING WITH FRESH EYES

Brainstorm ways you can participate more fully in public worship. Get creative, even unorthodox. The why of worship is worth it.

50

Sewing Machines

Give, and it will be given to you. A good measure,
pressed down, shaken together and running over,
will be poured into your lap. For with the measure
you use, it will be measured to you.
—LUKE 6:38

I should have never told anyone I could sew.
Despite legal blindness, I learned how to sew when I was a child. My family was of that generation when the only decent clothes were handmade. To say sewing was not my favorite choice of activity is too delicate. Who would enjoy getting a crick in the neck from being nose to needle for even an hour-long session? Freedom rang the day I put away my sewing machine for the last time.

And then Better Than Ever happened.

For several years, I belonged to a group that makes Christmas stockings for an outreach ministry to elderly folks in need in Romania. I dodged the sewing room by making midmorning treats and preparing lunch for the crew. Then I made the mistake of mentioning my former life. And someone remembered that little fact the day the sewing team was short of machine operators.

"You can see better now," the group coordinator said. "We need another person to run a sewing machine."

How could I say no? I'm the pastor's wife.

Biting back my angst, I sat, sewed a few stitches in my usual humped-over position, stopped, and stood up. "I need to go home to get my computer glasses."

I ran to my house next door and returned, emotion closing my windpipe at the emerging truth. The computer glasses confirmed my suspicion. *I could see to sew.* Well enough to sit straight instead of hunched. Well enough to see stitches and the fabric edge. Then I couldn't see at all because I was crying.

Later, Kim, the missionary, told how the elderly people in Romania received our gifts. Those dear people, who came from a culture that still valued handmade gifts, would caress their stockings and pray over them, thanking God and praying for the people who made them.

And I cried again.

Improved sight, God's gift to me, allowed me to give to others who did not have, even as I once did not have.

Everything we have is a gift. Everything. What we own, learn, and gain. Who we are and how we develop as we grow. Physical energy and health. Interests, passions, skills, and possessions. We can claim credit for none of it, for it all comes from God. We may not have as much as the person next to us, but we each have something we can give.

God asks us to give out of our storehouse, not the storehouse of our neighbor.

Just like he did for me, God can take an experience from your past, link it with what you have today, and then arrange for you to join others with their unique skills and talents from past and present. You and I and our co-laborers put it all together to offer a beautiful mixed bouquet to our God, inviting him to bless those in need in the name of Jesus through our combined efforts. Those who receive our sacrifice give thanks to the Giver and bless us with their prayers. And God takes all those actions we sometimes label as small and insignificant and does great and unimaginable things.

But some people are more skilled, have more, and know more than me, you may think. No matter. God asks us to give out of our storehouse, not the storehouse of our neighbor. Jesus told a parable of three servants who were entrusted with their wealthy master's money. To one, the master gave five bags of gold, the second received two bags, and the third, one bag (Matt. 25:14–30). The first two invested their money, but the third man hid his gold because he was afraid that whatever he did would not be good enough for his master. The master reproved him sharply for not investing what he had.

When we give even the smallest amount of what we have, God gives us more.

List what you call the weaknesses in your life. What golden thread of strength do you find embedded within those weaknesses? God is not asking you to do everything. He merely wants you to try your best when he asks, be available when he needs you, and give from what you have so he can bless others through you. It may not be much, and it may not be as much as what someone else gives. Give it anyway. Give it back to the God who gave it to you and who, through his unlimited strength, can do far more with that little bit than you could begin to think possible.

God in his heaven will smile.

Lord, I surrender everything I have to you—my strengths and my weaknesses. Use whatever you want to proclaim your message of love and peace to those who need to hear and see.

SEEING WITH FRESH EYES

What is God currently calling you to do that you've been resisting? Assess what you have and what God has to work with. Decide on a way you can bless others with the gifts, experiences, connections, and renewals God has given to you.

51

The Past

Jesus replied, "No one who puts a hand to the plow and looks back is fit for service in the kingdom of God."
—LUKE 9:62

New eyesight demanded I change the way I view my world. It challenged me to alter lifelong habits like how close I held a book to my face or using my sense of touch to guide a sharp knife along an apple core. Early in life, I had received training in adaptive skills for the blind, but no one offered suggestions this time on how to adapt to better vision. I was on my own to figure it out, and some days I didn't want to think about change.

I'd spent a lifetime developing coping mechanisms; couldn't I keep doing what I always did? My brain grew tired of reminding my arms to pull the book back, or telling my shoulders to straighten and my eyes to look at the knife blade. *You have two eyes; use them.*

No, one eye. Only one eye was better now. My right eye that could barely see the big *E* on eye charts was a constant reminder of how life used to be. One faded, blurred glance out of that crooked eye strengthened my resolve to pursue a future of seeing my world with new sight.

The Israelites felt that pendulum swing between the old and the new when they left the mountain of God to head toward the land God had promised them (Num. 10:33–11:6). They started to compare what they didn't like about their desert journey to the better days of free fish and vegetable gardens they'd enjoyed in Egypt. Despite their enslavement there, the past had its pleasant moments. It's so tempting to be like the Israelites. When the present gets tough, our minds want to grasp the good ole days, forgetting that there are parts of the past best left behind.

The apostle Paul realized that following Jesus is not necessarily a choice between bad and good but between comfortable and surpassing awesomeness. Paul had experienced the best in fame, ambition, legalistic morality, and education this world had to offer. After he met Christ, he was willing to let it all go, even if it meant experiencing a small share in the suffering of Jesus, because he knew something greater was waiting for him at his life's end (Phil. 3:4–11). Paul was determined to put distance between him and his past so he could draw closer to his goal of knowing Jesus (v. 10).

Taking hold of the eternal is worth the temporary loss of the past and its pleasant moments. I don't want to go back to a life of dependency and frustration. Altering old habits in exchange for the ease of doing more with better vision is truly a small price to pay. Looking at an apple as I cut out the core is, if I care to admit it, so much easier and safer than doing it by feel. Deliverance from the fear of cutting myself is a wonderful trade-off, worth constantly reminding myself to keep my eyes open to watch what I'm doing.

Likewise, following Jesus is a learning curve. It takes practice to put others first, sacrifice self, give up the pleasures of self-indulgence, swallow hurtful words when someone treats us unfairly, or trust God in the wait rather than feasting on a diet of worry. A few new experiences will tell you and me that life really does get better when done God's way. Peace and selflessness taste better than petulance and self-absorption. Each time your spirit retreats into familiar, comfortable patterns or wishes you could tell someone exactly what you think of them, one look at your past and the damage your old-life comments caused can be enough to remind you that you don't want to live like that anymore.

A taste of the new life from heaven is worth the removal from the past.

When you're tempted to slide into old habits or shrink into the myopia of your own needs, look at your past and the consequences of your self-imposed choices. Do you really want to go back to enslavement in your figurative Egypt? It's not worth it, my friend. You have something so much better now. Choose to look forward. Fix your eyes on Jesus, who has eternity waiting for you. He is the one who promised you death-defying power to do great and mighty things in this life. You've already seen him at work and experienced the peace, joy, and forgiveness he offers. You know what it's like to see him more clearly. A taste of the new life from heaven is worth the removal from the past.

Do you really want to go back to the person you used to be?

Let it go. Press on toward the freedom found in seeing Jesus as he fully is.

Lord, while this life has its comforts and pleasures, the life you offer is so much better. Forgive me for the times I slip back into the old ways. Help me loosen my grip on the past so I can follow you into the future you have planned for me.

SEEING WITH FRESH EYES

What is something from your past you miss? The next time your former life looks particularly enticing, stop yourself. List the ways life is so much better now that you are in partnership with Jesus.

PART 6

SEEING BEYOND THE SEEN

52

Fast-Food Signs

For in this hope we were saved. But hope that is
seen is no hope at all. Who hopes for what they
already have? But if we hope for what we do not
yet have, we wait for it patiently.
—ROMANS 8:24–25

Fast-food signs and coffee shop menus were still a huge source of frustration even after Better Than Ever. I edged closer to the counter each time, trying to decipher the letters, but I just couldn't quite read them. The old annoyances of not being able to see like everyone else returned with a vengeance.

I didn't understand why it was bothering me so much. *Good grief, woman. Your sight is so much better. Be grateful for what you now have.*

I still stared. That last reminder about gratitude didn't help. My husband could read the menu, so I knew it was possible.

So close but not close enough.

And that was the issue. After Better Than Ever, I knew reading overhead menus was possible. And I couldn't quite do it.

I'd sat in my six-foot bubble for decades, oblivious. Reading a fast-food menu sounded as impossible as flying to the moon seemed to someone in the twelfth century. Now, like early developers of rockets, I had a glimpse of what could be. *If I just try a little harder*, I thought. I cleaned my lenses, put my glasses back on, and leaned over the counter. *A tad more vision and I could read that screen.*

Why did God give me only so much improvement in my vision? Why stop at 20/100? Why is it 20/80 on some days and not on most days? Why didn't God go all the way and give me 20/20 vision? Why didn't God motivate the surgeon to take care of the damage done in the right eye while he was at it?

What is perfect vision anyway? Even 20/20, the standard for normal, is limited. Jesus chose to stuff his divinity into the restrictions of a human body, and that meant taking on the boundaries of human sight. In heaven, we will all have vision far beyond the best of mortal eyesight. No physical healing in this life is complete because any miracle of healing is still trapped by earthly parameters. No one has experienced perfect health, physical fitness, or visual acuity.

It's true in the spiritual realm too. I look at the lives of godly women like Mother Teresa and Elisabeth Elliot, and I chafe that I am not more like them. Like Paul in Romans 7, I lament over all that I am not.

Telling me I'm only human when my humanness splatters all over the floor for everyone to see doesn't make me feel better. It's so true: The older we get, the more we realize we don't know. The closer I get to God, the more I recognize how much I don't understand about him. The more I learn about the life that faith could live in me, the greater my awareness of how far I have to go. When I reach my life's end, will I have the amount of faith, hope, and love God would like me to have?

Why doesn't God bring about complete transformation at the same time as our initial salvation? The presence of the Holy Spirit is a fraction of the intimate relationship we could have with God. Why can't I—why can't any of us—see more of God right now?

We're not there yet.

This might sound strange if you've had normal vision throughout your life, but my improved vision convinced me of how someone might be able to see better than I do and that having that level of vision would be a nice thing. Before Better Than Ever, I could not conceive how the person next to me could see better. Why on earth would someone need two eyes or depth perception? But now I've had a taste of what better vision can be, and I'm even more excited for all that I will see when I enter God's eternal kingdom.

Likewise, my current relationship with God gives me a peek into what an unending, unbroken relationship with him will look like. I'm not there yet, by any means, but I have tasted of Christ's salvation and love, and found that it is good. In fact, it is really wonderful. The goodness makes me long for more, and I press forward to know my Lord better. Why? Because now I know what is possible.

Are you frustrated at the lack of Spirit-controlled consistency in your life? You've sampled the peace that only God can give. You've seen him do great and marvelous things for you. You've traded in your defiance for contentment, contentiousness for peace, hate and anger for love. But you know, deep inside yourself, you have so much further to go, and you are frustrated by the inconsistencies.

Me too. And, though it might be hard to believe, Mother Teresa and Elisabeth Elliot probably felt that way as well. As much as our ability to see God improves over our lifetime, we'll never have a full, clarified, face-to-face view or understanding of him until we reach heaven.

Consider the God glimpses and moments of intimacy as a deposit for what is yet to come.

In the meantime, consider the God glimpses and moments of intimacy as a deposit for what is yet to come. Keep looking for those sweet spots when God and you are in perfect sync. As time passes, those will become more numerous.

No, my friend, you are not there yet, but you are getting closer each day. And some day, you will fully know him as he has fully known you (1 Cor. 13:12).

That is the essence of eternity with God.

Lord, thank you for the God glimpses you give me, glimpses of what you're doing and how you are working to change my life. I long for more, but I take them now as a guarantee of what is yet to come.

SEEING WITH FRESH EYES

What is one spiritual area in which you've grown? What is something you wish you were better at? Thank God for your growth, and ask him to help you continue to grow.

53

Beyond Myself

Praise be to the God and Father of our Lord Jesus
Christ, the Father of compassion and the God of
all comfort, who comforts us in all our troubles, so
that we can comfort those in any trouble with the
comfort we ourselves receive from God.
—2 CORINTHIANS 1:3–4

It's one of those quirks of life. There's a name for it—frequency illusion. It's that tendency to see new words, ideas, or objects repeatedly after our initial introduction to them. You learn a new vocabulary word; you see it in print three times over the next few days. You buy a car make and model you think isn't trending; suddenly that same car is everywhere.

That could have been the case with my retina surgery. But I don't think so. Four acquaintances needing retina surgery a month after mine was too uncanny to be coincidental.

Sharon, a longtime friend of my family, came into my Facebook life six months before the Better Than Ever surgery. That itself was unusual because Sharon and I had never met each other. Yet, not long after Better Than Ever, Sharon told me she was to have retina surgery too.

My heart squeezed with compassion. I had wet-paint experience of the before, during, and after of a retina repair. I knew how the long, boring hours facedown on a couch would be tough but necessary.

How to help? First lesson: commiseration is not comfort. How many of us have experienced that well-meaning person who told us their surgical horror stories? The underlying message was, "You think *you* are bad off? Here's what happened to me."

God offers hope in three ways: his Word, the actions modeled by Jesus, and the provision of the Holy Spirit who walks beside us. We, in turn, pass forward the blessing of hope through our words, actions, and prayers for those who also need God's comfort.

I wanted to give hope to Sharon. I wanted her to see that regaining her vision was possible and that, in the meantime, she could endure the long wait, and I wanted to empower her with resources that would ease the waiting. I wanted to partner with her in imploring the Lord to do for her what he had so graciously done for me. Sharon and I both believed to the soles of our feet that God had brought us together so she could have someone in her life who had walked that journey before her.

Extending comfort is often not that textbook simple. I've watched several friends who were steadily, silently losing their vision from macular degeneration drop their gaze whenever I told my story, and my exuberance over my improved sight would fade. My gain magnified their loss, and I didn't want that. People enter our lives with a level of heartache we cannot begin to imagine, and sometimes our mere presence causes them to feel so alone. Too often they ask themselves, *Does anyone understand?*

How can we possibly comfort someone who has had an abortion, gone through a divorce, dealt with a child on drugs, or faced cancer if we've never experienced those things ourselves? Or what kind of help are we when we coast through a mild case of a disease and someone else faces life-threatening complications? What do we say when our marriage is restored and our best friend's marriage lies shattered, beyond repair?

I can't relate so I can't help, I tell myself. And my helplessness siphons my joy.

Or can I help? Can you? Have we walked any part of the path they travel? What *do* we possess that could give hope and show compassion?

Although my vision is better now, I spent over fifty years labeled as legally blind, attempting to achieve normalcy through unconventional means. While I discovered that independent living was possible with limited vision, I also gained the crucial, core understanding that God walks with us in the darkest moments. That one truth is a common-ground message we can confidently share with anyone: *You are not alone, and you will get through this.*

> You may not have experienced the same issue as your hurting friend, but you can still give the gift of hope.

You may not have experienced the same issue as your hurting friend, but you can still give the gift of hope. Second Corinthians 1:5 says, "For just as we share abundantly in the sufferings of Christ, so also our comfort abounds through Christ." The tough times allow you to identify with what Christ went through on the cross and access the endurance he makes available to you. That's the assurance you can pass forward to your suffering friend.

If you can't specifically relate with your friend's particular trial, admit it. Say, "I don't know what it's like to be in your situation, but here's something that helped me in a tough moment." Better yet, use your friend's struggle as your own teachable moment. Ask, "Tell me what it's like. Help me understand." Then listen. And pray. Confess to the Lord that, in your humanness, you don't know all the answers, but you know he does and that he has the power and motivation to help.

Your listening ear, your choice to share their suffering, may be the best comfort you can give.

*Lord, my friend is facing a time of anguish. Show
me how to relate so I can extend the same comfort
you have given me.*

SEEING WITH FRESH EYES

If you have experienced God's provision, protection, and presence in the midst of your story, ask God to show you how you can use that to encourage someone else walking a similar path.

54

Tears

For the Lamb at the center of the throne will be their shepherd; "he will lead them to springs of living water." "And God will wipe away every tear from their eyes."
—REVELATION 7:17

I'm good at shedding tears. Happy, sad, or touched by a tender, poignant story—it doesn't matter. The tears creep over the edges of my eyelids. They even had to demand center stage when I picked my new prescription glasses ten weeks after the Better Than Ever surgery.

It was early afternoon as I sat in the chair in the optical gallery. I swiveled my head. Jack's time-etched face, bearing a closed-mouth grin of anticipation, filled my vision. Up to this point, I'd taken him at his word that his eyes were brown; now I could see the color for myself. The image blurred.

"I can't see anything now," I said, taking off my new glasses and wiping my eyes.

The optician's laugh spoke of delight in a special moment. I apologized for the tears. She handed me a tissue and shrugged off my words. "These happy moments are the best part of my job," she said.

Why do we cry when we're happy or deeply touched? I'm working to figure that out. The biblical reassurance that God will wipe every tear from our eyes doesn't help (Rev. 21:4). What does God do with happy tears?

My excited human self wanted to loiter on the way home to count how many utility poles I could see at one time, inspect roadside wild-flowers, and observe moving clouds. But we had responsibilities waiting for us, and the car never slowed. We were slated to help at a children's program at our church that evening. As I greeted children in the pre-school class, one five-year-old girl stomped into the room, a fierce look on her face.

"She might be upset tonight," her mother warned. "The chains holding our two miniature pinschers tangled, and one of the dogs choked to death. Both our kids saw it happen."

The little girl grew more petulant as we moved from one activity to the next. Suddenly she exploded in anger. I pulled her aside and onto my lap.

"My dog died today," she whimpered.

"I know, honey." I tucked a stray lock of hair behind her ear. "It's okay to be sad."

Then I saw it: a gleaming, light-reflecting, grief-infused droplet resting on her cheekbone. Earth's sorrow stained her innocent skin. She had seen the finger of death that afternoon—something no five-year-old should see, something many of us do not witness until we've matured. In fact, God never intended any of us to see death; it wasn't part of his original plan.

I stared at that bit of pain-laced moisture. I had never seen a tear on someone's face before. Captivated by the beauty of a teardrop, I temporarily forgot what it represented—the suffering little girl sitting on my lap. Then I remembered.

In that moment I loved this child who had seen ugly things. I loved her as God's creation, a complete package, emotions included. I loved her enough to want to remove her heartache. I reached toward her face and transferred the tear to my fingertip.

Tear removal is an intimate gesture restricted to parents, family, and a privileged few allowed close enough to see our pain. If we are within touching distance to the tear, we're close enough to see the hurt.

Jesus promised to wipe all tears from our eyes once we enter heaven's courts. That means we'll be close enough for Jesus to touch us. He'll gather us in his arms and tenderly use his divine thumb to wipe away our tears. Like healing those with leprosy, he will dare to touch the untouchable, the emotion we would rather hide. He will bear on his person our deepest feelings and our greatest pain.

That's how much God loves you.

Why will tears stain our faces at the sight of heaven? Will they be happy or sad tears? No matter. Either represents release. In our more resolute moments on earth, we move through our days, trusting God's strength to get us through and clamping our lips together, determined not to have something to cry about. But we all have experienced the chains of suffering that choke the life and freedom out of us. The depravity of this earth is so commonplace, we easily forget that life could be lived any other way. And we stifle our tears at the sight of loss because it's become our normal and shouldn't bother us enough to cry about it.

But God knows. He never wanted life on this earth to go in the direction it did. He had something better in mind from the beginning. Knowing how sin would disrupt his original design, he set in motion the plans that will ultimately restore earth to its foundational purpose.

God is close enough to see and wipe away all your shed and unshed tears.

The instant you step into eternity, you'll see the Better Than Ever God had planned for you and all that it entails. You'll look beyond the Lord's shoulder at the life he intended all of us to have before Satan messed with Adam and Eve in the garden of Eden. And I suspect you and I will weep with both pain and joy. We'll ache with the realization of how life could have been not so hard and with the relief that the hard moments are gone forever.

What about the here and now? No matter what you are experiencing, God is close enough to see and wipe away all your shed and unshed tears. He already knows about what makes you cry or what you wish you could cry about. He sees the hurt. He stays near when others edge away, unaware or uncaring of how they've wounded you. He knows about your longings, how you wish life could be different. He hears the goodbyes and wants to tell you of the hellos that await you. Your loss is not permanent, and he's got the biggest, bestest surprise for you that you cannot even begin to imagine.

When no one else is near enough to hear or when shame or pride clamps your mouth shut and clogs your tear ducts, turn toward your heavenly Father so only he can hear and see you. Confide in him what you can tell no one else. Tell him your hurt, what made you sad, and how you wish life could be different. He already knows anyway. He cares. And he's got a plan to restore the losses of your life and bring justice to those parts of our world that have caused you to cry. As your Creator, heavenly Father, and Redeemer, God has earned the title of Tear Wiper and Counselor.

And he's promised that, one day, he will wipe clean your tears—the old and the new. In that simple gesture, he will remove all the feelings of anguish, guilt, and regret, touch your soul with his grace, and set you forever free from earth's tyranny. He'll rejoice with your happy tears that it's over now, the time has come to enter the joy of his kingdom, and relationship with you is restored to what he meant it to be in the first place.

The happy moment of wiping away your tears is the best part of his job.

Lord, you are a God who chose to come close,
pay the price to remove my pain, and take the
initiative to touch my tears. Thank you.

SEEING WITH FRESH EYES

Lean in close to your heavenly Father. Tell him what you can tell no one else. Keep a box of tissues handy. It's okay if you use a few.

55

Communion Cups

*"He himself bore our sins" in his body on
the cross, so that we might die to sins and live for
righteousness; "by his wounds you have
been healed."*
—1 PETER 2:24

If you'd asked me what I wanted to see the most once I healed from surgery, I would have told you Communion cups. In my church, we pass the trays down each aisle. As my vision waned before the Better Than Ever surgery, I couldn't tell the difference between a full cup and an empty cup, so with a blush I admitted my problem to Fergy, Carol, and Gloria. Each Sunday, one of these dear friends moved to sit beside me so they could silently point out the cup I needed to select.

I still felt uncomfortable. Dependence wasn't the issue. I wanted to think about Jesus more than whether I ran the risk of spilling grape juice on my white slacks or whether I was holding up the entire worship service by faltering over a Communion tray. If Better Than Ever would help me see Communion cups again, that would be lovely.

The Sunday after I picked up my new glasses prescription, Fergy handed me the tray, her finger pointing to a full cup. With an inaudible gasp of delight, I waved off her hand. I could see the cup in front of me. Joy flooded my whole being. The miracle was real.

The next Communion service, I pushed my limits. How much detail could my new vision catch? Oh, praise my precious Lord, I could see full cups on the far edge of the large round tray. That was much better than before the retina surgery. Wonder flooded over me yet again: he who had given his own Son had indeed graciously given me all things (Rom. 8:32). What sweet Communion. As I raised the cup to my lips, I articulated the meaning behind the ancient word *Eucharist*: "Thank you. Thank you, thank you."

My eyes saw the tray. My spirit saw Jesus. He was real. He was personal. He was the one who orchestrated the gift of Better Than Ever eyesight. From that day forward, Communion cups would remind me of God's power and love. *I once was blind but now I see.*

Was this how Eutychus felt after Paul, by God's power, brought him back to life? Acts 20 tells the story: Paul had gathered with the believers at Troas to break bread, the common expression for Communion. First, however, Paul spoke to them, and by the author's own assessment, the long-winded preacher "kept on talking" till midnight (v. 7). Eutychus, sitting in an open third-floor window, fell asleep and reeled to his death. Paul went downstairs, wrapped his arms around the young man, and announced, "He's alive!" (v. 10). Then they went back upstairs and broke bread.

Imagine Eutychus's feelings as he partook of the bread and wine that evening. *I was dead but now I'm alive.* The power of Christ had brought him back to life, the very same power that raised Jesus after his death on the cross. Imagine Eutychus, sixty years later, being called upon to give a Communion meditation and how he would have eagerly shared the sweet story of life from death.

Yes, we know, Eutychus and I, that by the wounds of Jesus, we are healed. This good news is for you too. For the same power that gave me sight, Eutychus life, and Jesus dominion over sin can heal the damage sin has done to your life. His forgiveness will restore your broken relationship with God. The sacrificial gift on the cross of his life for yours will free you to step into a new way of life and release you from all that is holding you apart from knowing him.

The bread and the wine of Communion allow you and me to see both our sin and God's solution to our sin.

The bread and the wine of Communion allow you and me to see both our sin and God's solution to our sin. They invite us to peer to the far edge of earthly life toward God's promised rescue from eternal death. His willingness to face the darkness floods our lives with Better Than Ever light.

What an awesome thing God has done for us—for you, for me. We are alive. We can see. And we will live forever because Jesus allowed his body to be broken and his blood to be spilled out of his great love for us. He truly has blessed us with every spiritual blessing found in Christ (Eph. 1:3).

Are you filled with awe yet? He did this for you! If you are having trouble grasping the enormity of the cross, do this the next time you participate in Communion: Reflect on what you have become because of Jesus. How do you see differently now that you have aligned your life with his? How has he freed you from the bondage of your past? How does it feel to know God has forgiven you of everything you've done wrong and he loves you enough to let you try again, this time with his help and his presence with and within you?

As you lift up that cup, praise him with a fresh sense of joy. For through the death of Christ, you can now see, you have new life, and you are free. God has found you and is bringing you home. Claim it and live in gratitude to the one who has given it.

Lord, because of what Jesus did for me, I can see
what lies in store for me on the other side of this

earthly life. Thank you, Father. Thank you for all
the spiritual blessings you have given to me.

SEEING WITH FRESH EYES

If you struggle with taking your salvation for granted, look at it through the eyes of someone who was blind but now can see, or as if you were dead and you've come back to life. How would you respond to that kind of freedom?

56

Westview Abbey

*I know that my redeemer lives, and that in the
end he will stand on the earth. And after my skin
has been destroyed, yet in my flesh I will see God;
I myself will see him with my own eyes—I, and not
another. How my heart yearns within me!*
—JOB 19:25–27

*J*n case you wondered, we did reach my mother-in-law's graveside
service in time that dreary December day when we raced from the
Atlanta airport to the cemetery. Afterward, Jack, the rest of his family,
and I drove the short distance to Atlanta's famous Westview Abbey
to pay honor to past family members. I had been to the mausoleum
before but never paid attention because, well, I couldn't see. When
family pointed out brass plates bearing names of people I didn't recognize or to particular touches of grandeur, I stared in the direction
they indicated and gave a cursory nod, hoping they wouldn't realize I
was faking.

This time, I noticed. At least I noticed the grandeur.

Built in 1943, Westview Abbey is one of the largest mausoleums
in the country. Its massive Spanish Renaissance architecture, detailed

with ornate doorways, windows, and facades, spreads over 150,000 square feet, a little over two and a half times the size of a football field. The exterior is made of molded cement, sculpted to look like carved stone. Gleaming tile floors fooled me with their marble look. Every hallway holds stained glass windows, stone slabs engraved with lines from famous poetry or Bible verses, and murals depicting scenes from Scripture.

I know because I could see it.

I saw crystal chandeliers hanging from the arched ceiling of the chapel. I craned my neck to study the rose window in the great hall. My eyes traced circles around doorway carvings and lingered over stained glass stories of the Good Shepherd and the Good Samaritan. And I wondered, *Why all this for a mausoleum?*

I must be too practical. Like some of the pragmatic bystanders who gasped at the price tag of the expensive perfume when a woman anointed Jesus's head before his crucifixion (Mark 14:1–9), I protested in silence, *Why artistic overload for a community mausoleum?*

Why not?

Jesus had a different reaction to the woman's gift: "She has done a beautiful thing to me" (v. 6). Using perfume instead of words, this unnamed woman spared no expense or cost to her reputation to honor the Lord she loved. Jesus had told his followers two chapters earlier that the law is wrapped up in this one command: "Love the Lord your God with all your heart and with all your soul and with all your mind and with all your strength" (12:30). Her act was living proof of what it means to love God with everything you have.

God made the world to be beautiful. He created us to be creative beings, to use everything we have within our being to imitate his creation of the beautiful to praise and honor our God, and to encourage others to do the same. Creative expression in all its various forms flows out of our emotions, intellect, and experience. We package all that together and get stunning work—the art of Michelangelo, the music of Bach, and the halls of Westview Abbey.

Yet there is more behind the why of Westview Abbey. Its artwork made me pause to consider the important fact that life doesn't finish at a dead end. Murals and stained glass pictures proclaimed Jesus, his power and love, and his plan to provide a way to a heavenly eternity. Verses in calligraphy, written in a giant-sized font on marble-like walls, caught my eye faster than if someone had placed an open Bible at a podium.

God created beauty to encourage us and draw us closer to him.

Beauty softens the sting of our struggle and attracts our hungering souls, communicating truth at a frequency within our listening range. In a thousand different ways, the soul surrendered to God learns to articulate the message: *Hope reigns.* God created beauty to encourage us and draw us closer to him.

Framed by the right time and place, creative expression speaks loudest in seasons of struggle and suffering. Think about what was happening in 1943, the year Westview Abbey was built. Immersed in World War II, mothers and fathers and sisters grappled with the why behind calamity and uncertainty. They buried sons too young in cemeteries tucked into the world's quiet corners. That generation needed reminders of hope. Their spirits looked for reassurance and comfort. And so the creative brain trust of Westview Abbey graced the walls, windows, and doorframes of that extravagant building with glimpses of God's glory, messages of heaven, and treasures of God's truth. They expressed what their audience needed to hear in ways they were ready to hear.

You and I need reminders too. Death plays no favorites. Each generation stands at the edge of the grave, asking why and how long till we meet again. Sorrow and loss rip the words and rationality from us, but God has other methods to call us back to himself, and he'll do anything to get our hearts in tune with his. What we may not catch in a sermon, we'll hear in a song or see in a mural.

The next time your heart is weary or broken, search for God's love notes through your favorite art form. Allow yourself to lament to God through music, art, dance, or poetry. Engross yourself in praise music, stand in awe of a nature scene, or find new ways to appreciate form, line, and perspective. Read the poetry of the Psalms.

God has given you these creative tools. Perform for him alone, or snuggle up close to him to appreciate their message with him.

That afternoon, I stood in the Westview Abbey chapel, turning in a circle and rotating my head up, down, and sideways. Unlike clouds or hummingbird wings, the beauty surrounding me was made by people, displaying humanity's creative expression of hope in something beyond death, a message anyone entering those halls needed to hear and see.

"You have a lovely voice," my cousin Gaye commented. "There's no one here. Why don't you sing?"

I opened my mouth to articulate the confidence I've found that smooths my path during troubled journeys. The perfect acoustics carried my song to the fluted ceiling and wrapped the melody around columns, lending a vibrato and clarity to my voice that allowed it to be at its best in praise of my God, and releasing my soul to express my rock-solid belief in the God who had already conquered death. In that moment of musical and visual beauty, my sagging spirit found reassurance in the highest of hopes.

Has sorrow, anger, confusion, or weariness gripped you by the throat? Do joy and excitement leave you speechless? Embrace the arts. God made music, color, rhythm, motion, and language in infinite varieties as his gift to you so you can replicate and appreciate the beautiful. Express it. Listen to it. Let it tell you the sweet story of Jesus and his love in a fresh way you may not have considered before. Use it lavishly to proclaim praise to your Creator and Redeemer, who bends close to earth to satisfy the longing soul.

Who knows? Someone might walk through the halls of your life and be touched and renewed by your creative expression of the hope you find in Jesus.

Father, I want to draw closer to you through the
trials I face. Help me to voice the truths I discover
in creative, beautiful ways that convey your gift of
hope to those around me.

SEEING WITH FRESH EYES

Choose your favorite art form—singing, drawing, coloring. Enjoy or create something that expresses your trust in God. This is for you and God alone. Don't fret about perfection; just offer it to him as your love gift for all that he means to you.

57

The Lord

God did this so that they would seek him and
perhaps reach out for him and find him, though he
is not far from any one of us.
—ACTS 17:27

Some days I can see better than other days. Now that I've experienced better days, bad days are annoying.

Sometimes the solutions are simple. Turn on the light. Move closer. Look in the right direction. Clean my glasses and use artificial tears.

My life has moments too when God seems far away and his voice is silent. Other believers tell of God sightings, and I chafe that I didn't notice. My daily Bible reading looks like nothing more than a page of jumbled letters, and prayer appears to bounce off the ceiling.

Do you have days when your view of God seems more distorted than usual, or worse yet, you can't find God at all?

Isaiah told of seeing the Lord, high and lifted up, his glory overflowing the boundaries of the temple (Isa. 6:1). Moses spoke to God face-to-face as to a friend (Exod. 33:11). The apostle John struggled for words to describe in the book of Revelation all that he saw in heaven's domain.

And I see dirty dishes, stacks of mail, sad faces, a lengthy to-do list, and a longer prayer list full of unfulfilled requests. *Where is God? Why can't I see him?*

Sometimes, the solutions are simple.

Turn on the light. God's Word is like a lamp, shedding light on our daily path (Ps. 119:105). If some parts of the Bible don't make sense, keep reading. Take notes. Be intentional. As you read more, the light will brighten and your understanding of how to navigate the more obscure parts of life will grow.

Move closer. Look for God. Talk to him about everything. Involve him in every part of your life. Tell him, *I want to see you.* Ask, *Where are you? Show me.* As the author of Hebrews instructed, "Let us then approach God's throne of grace with confidence, so that we may receive mercy and find grace to help us in our time of need" (4:16). Did you catch the *confidence* word? That means you don't need to hesitate or press your back against the wall, thinking God is too busy to notice you. Step right up, my friend. He wants to visit with you.

Look at God with truth and accuracy. Humanity has had two thousand years to spin misconceptions of who Jesus is and what he did while he resided on earth. When you use any of those philosophies as a starting point, your perception of Jesus will be as out of line as if you put on a pair of glasses with the wrong refraction. Don't be afraid to question what others have said or written about God. Ask yourself, *Is that really true?* Use critical thinking to dissect what you hear and then bring the idea under the light of what you are learning in your Bible reading. Ask God for the clarity of wisdom and the courage to speak and live truth.

Clean the clutter and remove the grime. Distractions abound every day. I can't seem to get through five minutes of prayer without random thoughts dogging my conversation with my God. Is your prayer life like that? Like the thorns that choked the seed in the parable of the sower (Matt. 13), worries and earthly pleasures can impede your view of God. If you want to see God better, step away from the intruders. Unhealthy friendships? Anxious thoughts? Too many commitments?

If they hinder your ability to get closer to God, move them out of the way.

But sometimes the solutions don't look simple. Perhaps the stresses of life have formed a tight circle around you, demanding your undivided, immediate attention. How can you move close to God when all those demands threaten to block your view of him?

If you claim Christ, God is with you and within you always.

God is nearer than you realize. He is not far from any of us (Acts 17:27). Even in Old Testament times, God promised to be with his people. In the Christian era, he imparted his Holy Spirit to live within every believer. If you claim Christ, God is with you and within you always. No catastrophe is too large, no list of demands too long, to push him out of view. He is entwined with your life, even in—especially in—the midst of your storm.

I've seen the glory of God in the delicate details found in creation and the power of God expressed in the lives of those I love. I've witnessed his presence in both the ordinary and the chaotic. You can see him too. He is present in the dark seasons of despair and in the light-filled moments of deliverance. He shines bright in suffering as well as in the spectacular. He will never leave you, never abandon you. He is there. And he is awesome. He longs to let his glory overspill the boundaries of your life.

He is a God who wants to be seen, and if you are willing to step toward him, he will show you more of himself.

Lord, I want to see you, your glory, your power,
and your mercy. I give you permission to show me
the solutions I need to apply in my life so I can get
a better view of you.

SEEING WITH FRESH EYES

Start your day by asking God to give you a peek of himself. Choose one of the suggestions offered above and intentionally look for God. At the day's end, record what you've discovered.

58

Heaven's Threshold

That is why I am suffering as I am. Yet this is no cause for shame, because I know whom I have believed, and am convinced that he is able to guard what I have entrusted to him until that day.
—2 TIMOTHY 1:12

When Anne, an older lady in our women's fellowship group, entered hospice, my friend Cyndy and I both felt a sense of urgency. We drove the thirty-five miles to her care facility, hoping we were not too late. When we reached Anne's bedside, I held her hand and assured her that God loved her and was with her. To my ears, the words sounded hollow and perfunctory.

Not to Anne. "Oh, he's here," she said with a ring of utter conviction.

My mind raced. Should I take her literally? Was Anne so far along her journey to the end that she could see heaven's light? Was she having one of those wonderful near-death experiences I've only read about? Curiosity overcame sensible caution, and I gathered the gall to ask, "What do you see, Anne? Do you see Jesus?"

"No." The pause was contemplative. "But I know he's here."

We asked Anne if we could sing her favorite hymn. She thought for a moment, then began to sing it herself. We let her, filling in words she stumbled over. Her voice held reverence, conviction, and unadulterated adoration. Jesus was real. She didn't have to see him to know he was there.

I should have known. My years of limited vision should have reminded me. I don't need eyesight to identify my environment. Blind and visually impaired people can quickly tell the difference between a closed walkway and an open space by listening to the sounds. White canes give a data bank of information about terrain, slopes, and steps. I don't have to see to know.

Seeing is believing, the old maxim says. God's Word says differently. Faith is defined by the confidence we have in what we hope for (Heb. 11:1). Faith removes the wistful wish and the shrug of uncertainty when we express our expectation for a Better Than Ever eternity. We can't see Jesus, but our spirits sense his presence as much as our flesh feels the brush of a breeze-filled day. Just as a running line of dancing leaves indicates the presence of an invisible wind, so we can tell that God has been there, working his wonders in ways only he can do.

Faith puts in check the doubts of today with the recollection of how God showed up in the past.

Anne knew Jesus was real because she had spent most of her life sitting at his feet, and she had seen that he was good (Ps. 34:8). Faith holds fast to long-term memory, for faith puts in check the doubts of today with the recollection of how God showed up in the past. It remembers the promises and the promises fulfilled. It recounts those moments when the impossible turned into reality and recalls how life changed when our rebellion morphed into righteousness.

Faith is content not to ask for signs and wonders as proof of Jesus's divinity. His Word and the testimony of those who accurately predicted his coming are enough to convince us of his reality, plans, and care for us.

You can have that level of confidence. It's not an arrogant delusion to say you know when you don't have visible proof. Hope is a confident assurance that something will happen even if you cannot see it. Like a child who is brazenly certain she will have a birthday party because her parents have always given one before, so Anne could say with utter assurance that God would stay with her through the toughest part of her life journey. God had always been there before, and he was far more reliable than any set of parents.

Go ahead. Give yourself permission to say you know Jesus is real, even though you can't see him. Have the courage to say it out loud to other believers and the not-so-sure believers. God made the world and sent his Son to earth to die a sacrificial death for those who believe in him, even if you weren't there to watch it. God will keep his promises, even if you can't see his behind-the-scenes preparations. You have a blessed eternity with your Lord waiting for you, even if you haven't had a near-death experience to prove it. It's waiting for you if you have the faith to say you know it's true and you're willing to act on that faith.

As we held her hands to say goodbye, Cyndy told Anne we would come back to see her.

"I won't be here," Anne said. She was convinced. And so were we. Jesus was there to take her home.

Lord, I believe in you, but sometimes my
confidence wobbles. Help me grow to know a solid
reassurance of your care, love, and plan for me,
even if I don't see it.

SEEING WITH FRESH EYES

Whisper these sentences to yourself several times throughout the rest of your waking day: *Jesus is real. He keeps his promises. He has heaven waiting for me.*

59

Not Enough

I want to know Christ—yes, to know the power of
his resurrection and participation in his sufferings,
becoming like him in his death.
—PHILIPPIANS 3:10

After over fifty years of severely limited sight, I have some catching up to do. If I could drive, I'd head out for a three-month tour of places I've never seen, as well as places I've only seen dimly. Yosemite. The Grand Canyon. Niagara Falls. The Catalina Mountains north of my childhood home.

The more I discover, the more I realize how much I've missed. The experiences of dirt and bathroom scales have taught me to appreciate the small and ordinary in addition to the big and beautiful, but that has only lengthened my already long bucket list. I want to visit a botanical garden, stare into the face of a dolphin at an aquarium, and ride in a helicopter. My aging body taunts me with the brevity of time as I wonder if I'm too old to hike a mountain canyon, ride a bike without falling off, play basketball, or endure a trip to a foreign land.

It's wonderful, this seeing thing. I want to make up for all the missed moments, those times I went places and faked that I could see what everyone else saw. Sometimes the longing is so great, I feel like I could crawl out of my skin. *Why would God give me such a wonderful gift of new sight only to keep me penned up at home during an ice storm*, my late-winter irritability wants to whine.

Stop. Just stop.

Am I as driven to know God as I am in my desire to see?

Even more, is it worth an all-out, unrestrained effort to look for God?

The message of a parable Jesus once told is yes, it is. Pursuit of God is worth everything you have. Jesus compared the kingdom of heaven to a pearl of such great value that a man sold everything he owned in order to have it (Matt. 13:45–46). That sounds like far more commitment than my eagerness to dump my day job for three months so I could check off items on a world-tour bucket list. How much am I willing to give up for God?

How much are you?

And practically speaking, what does that look like in the everyday moment?

How do you make God a priority at your job?

What do you need to replace in your home life?

What kind of vacation can you take to nurture your relationship with God or share the wealth of your faith with others?

What activity are you willing to stop in the middle of doing so you can tell a stranger how God has changed your life?

Let me tell you what can happen. The results are so amazing, you want to do it again. And again and again. You're ready to sign up for another short-term mission trip. The sweet fellowship of family devotions brings more pleasure than everyone sitting in their own corner, doing their own thing. Watching someone take the final steps toward salvation when you had a direct part in their journey to faith will embolden you to go out and find someone else you can influence to accept God's message of grace.

I've had a taste of that. New eyesight has shown me more of who God is and how he views life, creation, and the people he's made and loved. Every time someone pauses in wonder and praise of God's power because they've heard my story of improved sight, I have this deep, core-level satisfaction and an overwhelming impulse to go tell my story again.

The more I see of God, the more I want to know. I want to see more examples of what he has done. I want to spend more time with this incredible God.

Let's be like the deer panting for water, convinced it will die if it doesn't get that life-replenishing drink (Ps. 42:1). Like the woman who met Jesus at a well and was attracted to his offer of living water (John 4). Ah, water that would take away all thirst. Let's find treasures in his Word, see more souls saved, and watch how God transforms lives and lifts up the fallen.

Yet here is what I find in Scripture. If we want to know and understand all God's facets, we must also be willing to experience his suffering in order to appreciate his might and his love. Only then will we know his heart. Being that in tune with God would be wonderful, because when we are, Paul promises in Philippians 3:10, we'll see and experience firsthand the level of power Jesus felt when he was raised from the dead.

The depths of the riches of God's wisdom are so unfathomable, you'll never reach the extent of them.

But then there's that bit about suffering. I have days when I falter in my commitment to know Jesus so well that I'm willing to endure pain, discomfort, social isolation, the disapproval of others, or even inconvenience. Maybe you do too. Knowing Christ in all his glory and fullness may mean dying to your old way of life, letting go of the past so you can reach for the new. Casting off your old prescription glasses so you can see as God does. Living such a new, different style of life that your friends and family reject you. The old is hard to put aside.

But if relinquishing my personal pleasures, going through the discomfort of change, even standing up for his honor at the risk of losing mine means experiencing Jesus's life-renewing power through the gift of eternity with him, isn't it so worth it?

What makes Jesus worth the search? He is beautiful. He is good. He is gracious. He is powerful, strong, caring, and lavish in love. The depths of the riches of God's wisdom are so unfathomable, you'll never reach the extent of them (Rom. 11:33). You will always have more to see. You'll never run out of new discoveries about this God of yours. The joy comes in that discovery, and as long as there is more to uncover, the excitement of exploration continues.

Are you ready? How much do you want to know God better? Let's keep looking for him. In the dirt, the sunset, the faces of those he's created. In the big and beautiful and the everyday and ordinary. Then let's turn what we see to a new angle and ask him to show us what he sees and how he sees it.

The look will make you want to see even more.

Lord, I'm showing up. I want to know you, and I'm
ready to do whatever it takes to see you as you
are. Lead me, I pray, to understand you better.

SEEING WITH FRESH EYES

Make the development of your relationship with God a priority. Carve out a section of today to spend time getting to know him better.

60

Enough

The eyes of all look to you, and you give them their
food at the proper time. You open your hand and
satisfy the desires of every living thing.
—PSALM 145:15–16

In my hunger to see more of God and his world, I've had to do some backtracking. Our younger daughter, Christine, reminded me of that when she came home to our rural town for a visit from the big city.

"You're so blessed," she said. "You can walk toward the sunset. You can see things I can't where I live: the night sky, flocks of birds, and the occasional fox. All I see are squirrels who eat my birdseed."

Her words made me pause. I needed to find the balance between longing for more and finding contentment in what I already had. And I do have so much. Each day of sight, of life, of relationship, is a gift. While it would be wonderful to add more check marks to my bucket list, I've learned to surrender my desires to the one who has orchestrated all that I've already seen. I've found joy in living in the everyday moment and in asking each morning, *Lord, what do you want me to see today?* He does such a better job as my tour guide than I do.

Yes, my current visual acuity is still far from normal. I can't shoot a basket, crochet fine lace, read normal print while standing at a speaker's lectern, or drive a car. Yet my sight is more than I ever dreamed of having in this lifetime. I see Better Than Ever.

More than that, I've gained a fuller, more accurate view of God. It feels like he's drawn me close to his side, put his arm around me, and shown me how to look at the world and other people the way he does. Seeing him and seeing what he sees has been the greater miracle.

He is the God of good and perfect gifts. He customizes them to fit who I am and what he has planned for me. While normal sight throughout life would have been nice, I am who I am, and my imperfect vision and jittering eyeballs are as much a part of me as my toothy smile, pert nose, and overactive tear ducts.

For that matter, I have other imperfections: etched cracks in the window of my soul where past sin and unintended consequences distorted my acceptance of a God who loves me lavishly. Those fault lines are there to stay until heaven's remaking. In the meantime, it's who I am, and God is so expert at using those imperfections to communicate his ways to those who know me and watch me. His grace fills the cracks and shines through me, reminding me and others that his strength is made perfect in my weakness (2 Cor. 12:9).

God's gift of enough protects me from the excessive pitfall of too much.

Why doesn't God give us all that we want? Why did he set the normal standard for sight, hearing, or strength where he did? Perhaps the limit is for our own protection. Children without boundaries run too far, explore too long, and get into areas with no escape route. God has placed sensory limitations on all of us for a reason. Seeing, hearing, or manipulating the world with unlimited energy would be overwhelming and ultimately implosive. With riches comes the responsibility to use the wealth wisely.

God's gift of enough protects me from the excessive pitfall of too much. I am content because I know my heavenly Father has designed the package of me to be just the right combination of strengths and weaknesses, abilities and deficiencies. What I am and what I have is enough; I really don't need any more.

The only thing I need more of is him and his likeness.

The apostle Paul longed for heaven's riches, but he found contentment in staying on earth because God needed him in the here and now (Phil. 1:22–26). I like Paul's attitude. If he went to heaven immediately, he couldn't continue his work of sharing the gospel and strengthening the churches he had established. Lingering on earth meant that when the time came for him to leave, he would take more saints with him. Joy multiplied.

If my current, still-limited visual status means greater good for God's glory, that's what I want. If a crisis or catastrophe, like Paul's time in prison, leads to the salvation of many, yes, bring it on. If a desperate need gives rise to a display of God's deliverance, all the better. And if my better vision is only a seasonal gift and I lose it later, that's all right. I'll be satisfied because I can be confident God has yet other plans that will bring him glory, and his glory is what I want most of all. Like Paul, I can be content because my hope rests in God, and he can work through whatever circumstances life presents.

The gift of enough is there for you too. God works within each life situation to show you and those watching that he is God and there is no other. He is worthy of our trust and worship. Whether he rescues you from the pain or walks with you through it, he will give you a story to tell that allows you to say, "See what God has done."

You may be reading my story and wishing you had more, thinking that your miracle wasn't big enough. Why would I get more sight and you are losing yours? Why do some get healing from cancer and your beloved didn't? Some get groceries delivered on their doorstep and others starve. Others find relief from their pain and yours is relentless despite medical intervention.

Remember, my vision is still far from what most consider normal.

But it is enough. It's exactly the amount God wants me to have right now. Enough to do what God has commissioned me to do. And, my friend, whatever circumstances you face, God can use them to do marvelous things within you and through you. Because we have such a creative God, your miracle and his provision for you may look vastly different from mine.

Approach what you face and what you are with the starting point that God is a good, good God who knows what is best for you. He has the power and love to do amazing things with whatever plans he has for you. You are precious to him, and your life, in whatever state it is in, can bring God honor. In that you can find satisfaction.

The best of the best will come in the form of heaven's halls, eternity with the Lord you love. Contentment and endurance are possible now because something so much better will soon be yours.

The best is yet to come. And that is enough.

Thank you, oh my good God, that you are all I
need. Thank you for making me as I am, gifting me
with what I have, and preparing Better Than Ever
for my final homecoming. I love you, Lord.

SEEING WITH FRESH EYES

Today, determine to focus on what you do have, not on what you don't have. Start your day by listing and thanking God for three things you have. If you catch yourself lingering on something you don't have, add two more things to your list for which you are thankful.

My Prayer for You

*I pray that the eyes of your heart may
be enlightened in order that you may
know the hope to which he has called
you, the riches of his glorious inheritance
in his holy people.*
—EPHESIANS 1:18

J'm praying for you. I pray that you will see Better Than Ever, that
you will see in new ways:

Who God is
What God has done
The world God has made
The people he has made and longs to bring home

I pray that you will see God in every moment:

In the ordinary and exciting
In the pleasant and heart-wrenching
In both the known and uncertain

No matter the level of your physical sight or the circumstances of your life, may you grow in your ability to see as God sees.

May you view life through his eternal perspective.

May you see people in the same way he sees them: lost but loved and longing for a final home that only he can provide.

May you find new insights in his Word, the Bible, that teach you how to follow after him and know him even better.

May you catch more frequent glimpses of his vision for the future of our world.

This journey of discovery will take a lifetime of ordinary moments. But as the Lord opens the eyes of your heart to see what he sees and how he sees it, the ordinary will become holy and miraculous. You'll realize that God reigns over each moment and that he is with you every step in your journey toward Better Than Ever.

Join me. Let's go find God together.

Read more of my discoveries on my website, www.karenwingate.com. And I'd love to hear about your Better Than Ever moments. Write me at karen@karenwingate.com.

Acknowledgments

So many people have served as sighted guides, both physically and spiritually, throughout my life that I would need to write another book to acknowledge each of these precious people. Human that I am, I would forget someone, and I do not want to do that. However, the following people deserve special thanks.

Foremost is my prayer team, who have prayed me through each speaking and writing venture. First there was the Significant Seven, and then there was the Team of Twenty. We learned together the power and beauty of extreme, specific prayer. We learned that in and of ourselves, we'll make a mess of things, but when we partner with God, the unimaginable can happen. And we also discovered that no successful ministry is a solo act. Any project takes a support team. This book is not my book; it is ours. Thank you to all who prayed me through the writing process.

Other special thanks go to:

Dr. Chittaranjan Reddy, who had the expertise to grasp the nature of my complicated eye condition and the initiative to do something about it during a surgical procedure. Thank you for speaking those hope-filled words, "Better Than Ever."

Dr. Jill Brody, whose confident and calm approach helped me many times to relax about the future of my eyesight. Thanks also to you and your staff for your good humor in putting up with my attempts to cheat on the eye chart.

Dr. Jack Cottrell, former theology professor at what was then Cincinnati Christian Seminary. Your simple, plain-words explanation about God's grace liberated me from trying to kill myself in my overdrive to earn my salvation.

My two precious daughters, Katherine and Christine, who have kept me both humble and encouraged by telling me I was "household famous." I'm so proud of these two young women who long ago surpassed me in pursuing compassion for others, discovering deep spiritual truths, and persevering through the tough stuff. Keep the faith, ladies.

The extended family of my childhood, who had the patience to keep pointing out God's wonders to me even when they knew I was faking when I said I could see the object they were pointing at just to make them happy.

My incredible church family, who still laugh when I offer to drive the church van.

My agent and friend, Linda Glaz of Hartline Literary Agency, who refused multiple times to let me give up. When my vision was at its worst, she threatened to have me dictate my manuscripts over the phone if that's what it took to keep me writing. You are forever my chief encourager. May God keep you encouraged as you have encouraged all of us.

My husband, Jack, whom I affectionately call Preacher Creature. You give me the dignity of walking in front of you even when I can't see where I'm going so I don't look blind or dependent, quietly calling out cues from behind so I know where to turn next. From the beginning, we held hands and everyone thought we were so romantic when, in truth, you were acting as my sighted guide. Even though I can see better now, I still want to hold your hand. Oh, and thanks for the chocolate, back rubs, computer bailouts, and, um, maybe the red ink spilled over my rough drafts.

Jean Shull, who left to live with Jesus a long time ago. You modeled how to live out joy and a personal faith despite multiple obstacles in your life. By becoming part of our family, you brought Jesus close enough for me to see that he is real and that faith in God could infuse every part of our weekday moments. Thank you for accepting me as I was and painting a picture of what I could become.

The faculty and staff at the 2017 SpeakUp Conference and the 2018 Maranatha Christian Writers' Conference. My ideas were still so rough-hewn, but when I told any faculty member my original concept for what would become this book, you responded with, "This is a great idea. This could go places!" That encouragement carried me forward in a time when I was discouraged about so many other things in my life. Thank you for inspiring me to keep moving forward.

The marketing and editing teams at Kregel Publications. You caught the message I was trying to convey, embraced it with excitement, and used the gifts God has given you to make it shine. This book is yours too.

And, oh, did I mention my prayer team? Keep praying, because God can do anything, and he loves it when we involve him in any part of our lives. His partnership is what turns the ordinary into the miraculous.